Echoes
of the
Sea

illustrated by Jean Vallario

poems selected by Elinor Parker

Echoes
of the
Sea

CHARLES SCRIBNER'S SONS   *New York*

Copyright © 1977 Elinor Parker

Library of Congress Cataloging in Publication Data
Main entry under title:
Echoes of the sea.
    Includes indexes.
    SUMMARY: A collection of poems by various authors
pertaining to the sea.
    1. Sea poetry. [1. Sea poetry]   I. Parker,
Elinor Milnor, 1906–   II. Vallario, Jean.   III. Title.
PN6110.S4E3   821'.008'032   76-54719
ISBN 0-684-14852-8

ACKNOWLEDGMENTS

The Editor and the Publisher gratefully acknowledge the following poets, agents, and publishers for per-
mission to reprint poems in this anthology. Every effort has been made to locate all persons having any
rights or interests in the material published here. If some acknowledgments have not been made, their
omission is unintentional and is regretted.

"Atlantis" by Conrad Aiken: From *Collected Poems* by Conrad Aiken. Copyright © 1953, 1970 by Conrad
Aiken. Reprinted by permission of Oxford University Press, Inc."

"Sea-Birds" by Elizabeth Akers: From *The Home Book of Verse*. Published by Holt, Rinehart and Win-
ston, Inc.

"Whale" by William Rose Benét: From *The Third Book of Modern Verse*, edited by Jessie B. Rittenhouse.
Reprinted by permission of Houghton Mifflin Company.

"Over the Green Sands" by Peggy Bennett (Cole): From *The Birds and the Beasts Were There*. Reprinted by
permission of Collins-World Publishers, Inc.

"The Sandpiper" by Witter Bynner: From *A Canticle of Pan* by Witter Bynner. Copyright © 1920 by
Alfred A. Knopf, Inc. and renewed 1948 by Witter Bynner. Reprinted by permission of Alfred A.
Knopf, Inc.

"Echoes," "Mermaids," "The Pool in the Rock," "The Storm," "Sunk Lyoness," by Walter de la Mare:
From *The Complete Poems of Walter de la Mare*. Reprinted by permission of The Literary Trustees of
Walter de la Mare and The Society of Authors as their representative.

"A Sea Song" by D. M. Dolben: From *The Poems of Digby Mackworth Dolben* edited by Robert Bridges
(2nd ed. 1915). Reprinted by permission of Oxford University Press.

"Sea-Hawk" by Richard Eberhart: From *Collected Poems 1930–1976* by Richard Eberhart. © 1976 by Rich-
ard Eberhart. Reprinted by permission of Oxford University Press, Inc., and Chatto and Windus Ltd.

"Neptune" and "Waves" by Eleanor Farjeon. "Neptune" copyright © 1960 by Eleanor Farjeon: From the
work entitled *The Children's Bells* published by Henry Z. Walck, Inc., a division of David McKay Com-
pany, Inc. Reprinted by permission of the publisher and of Oxford University Press. "Waves": From
Poems for Children by Eleanor Farjeon. Copyright 1951 by Eleanor Farjeon. Reprinted by permission of
J. B. Lippincott Company and Harold Ober Associates Incorporated.

Seven lines from "The Dying Patriot" and fourteen lines from "A Fragment" by James Elroy Flecker:
From *Collected Poems* by James Elroy Flecker published 1922 by Alfred A. Knopf, Inc. Reprinted by per-
mission of Alfred A. Knopf, Inc.

"Diver" by Robert Francis: From *Come Out into the Sun*. Copyright © 1936, 1964 by Robert Francis.
Reprinted by permission of the University of Massachusetts Press.

"Moon-bathers" by John Freeman. From *Music* published by Selwyn and Blunt, 1921.

"The Dancing Seal," "Green Shag," "The Ice-Cart," "Sea-Change," by Wilfred Gibson. Reprinted by
permission of Michael Gibson.

"The Flying Fish" by John Gray: From *The Cherry Tree*, compiled by Geoffrey Grigson. Published by
Phoenix House, 1959.

"The Curlew" by Sara Henderson Hay: Copyright 1944 by the New York Times Company.

"Tidal Pool" by Sara Henderson Hay: Copyright 1944 by Sara Henderson Hay, from the book *A Footing
on This Earth* by Sara Henderson Hay. Reprinted by permission of Doubleday & Company, Inc.

v

In Memoriam
R.M.P.
"Full Fathom Five"

Contents

Preface

ALL ANTHOLOGIES ARE more or less personal, even the standard classics like *The Golden Treasury* or *The Oxford Book of English Verse.* This is a very personal one, based on a life-long love of the seashore. My earliest recollection—I could have been only two at the time—is of running along the sand toward my mother who was wearing a white dress. At least part of every vacation since has been spent on the coast of Maine where at high tide the waves pound against the rocks, sending up foam and spray, and at low tide the rock pools hold treasures of sea anemones and starfish. As the tide goes out the little shore birds hunt for food and the gulls cry overhead.

Of astrology I know nothing beyond the fact that my sign is Pisces, the Fishes. My birthstone is the aquamarine, the color of sea water in the shallows. Perhaps these have been influences as well. Deep water, out of sight of land, I find inexpressibly tedious, so there are no poems here about "a life on the ocean wave" or jolly sailors. Ocean liners were thankfully exchanged for planes as soon as commercial transatlantic flights began, and seasickness became a thing of the past. I am, in fact, a landlubber and travel by sea only in imagination—which brings me to mermaids.

When I was about ten I was enrolled in a class for "interpretive" dancing. My mother made me a sea-green tunic, which I liked, but I was thoroughly bored with the dancing, except for one piece. The music, played by a piano accompanist, was a lovely, lilting waltz which I have never been able to identify although I can still hear it in my head; the poem we were supposed to "interpret" was "The Forsaken Merman" by Matthew Arnold. It captured and held me spellbound then and it still does, which is why in spite of its length it had to be included in this book. At about the same time, I discovered Hans Andersen's "Little Mermaid." This, too, inevitably brings tears.

Someone may say that Milton's Sabrina is ineligible as she was a river goddess. Her river, the Severn in western England, has a long tidal estuary, so if she was doing her job properly she must have been in salt water part of the time. All the personages in the poem's second verse are sea deities, starting with Oceanus himself. And who could resist that "amber-dropping hair."?

—E. P.

The
Great
Deep

boundless, endless and sublime,
The image of eternity.

—LORD BYRON

THE OCEAN

Roll on, thou deep and dark blue Ocean—roll!
Ten thousand fleets sweep over thee in vain;
Man marks the earth with ruin—his control
Stops with the shore; upon the watery plain
The wrecks are all thy deed, nor doth remain
A shadow of man's ravage, save his own,
When, for a moment, like a drop of rain,
He sinks into thy depths with bubbling groan,
Without a grave, unknell'd, uncoffin'd, and
     unknown. . . .

*   *   *

Thou glorious mirror, where the Almighty's form
Glasses itself in tempest; in all time,—
Calm or convulsed, in breeze, or gale, or storm,
Icing the pole, or in the torrid clime
Dark-heaving—boundless, endless, and sublime,
The image of eternity, the throne
Of the Invisible; even from out thy slime
The monsters of the deep are made; each zone
Obeys thee; thou goest forth, dread, fathomless, alone.

LORD BYRON

ON THE SEA

It keeps eternal whisperings around
    Desolate shores, and with its mighty swell
    Gluts twice ten thousand caverns, till the spell
Of Hecate leaves them their old shadowy sound.
Often 'tis in such gentle temper found,
    That scarcely will the very smallest shell
    Be moved for days from whence it sometime fell,
When last the winds of heaven were unbound.
Oh ye! who have your eye-balls vexed and tired,
    Feast them upon the wideness of the Sea;
        Oh ye! whose ears are dinned with uproar rude,
    Or fed too much with cloying melody,—
        Sit ye near some old cavern's mouth, and brood
Until ye start, as if the sea-nymphs quired!*

JOHN KEATS

THE TIDES

I saw the long line of the vacant shore,
    The sea-weed and the shells upon the sand,
    And the brown rocks left bare on every hand,
As if the ebbing tide would flow no more.
Then heard I, more distinctly than before,
    The ocean breathe and its great breast expand,
    And hurrying came on the defenceless land
The insurgent waters with tumultuous roar.

* choired

3

All thought and feeling and desire, I said,
    Love, laughter, and the exultant joy of song
    Have ebbed from me forever! Suddenly o'er me
They swept again from their deep ocean bed,
    And in a tumult of delight, and strong
    As youth, and beautiful as youth, upbore me.

HENRY WADSWORTH LONGFELLOW

THE SOUND OF THE SEA

The sea awoke at midnight from its sleep,
    And round the pebbly beaches far and wide
    I heard the first wave of the rising tide
    Rush onward with uninterrupted sweep;
A voice out of the silence of the deep,
    A sound mysteriously multiplied
    As of a cataract from the mountain's side
    Or roar of winds upon a wooded steep.
So comes to us at times from the unknown
    And inaccessible solitudes of being,
    The rushing of the sea-tides of the soul;
And inspirations, that we deem our own,
    Are some divine foreshadowing and foreseeing
    Of things beyond our reason or control.

HENRY WADSWORTH LONGFELLOW

ICEBERGS
from **The Rime of the Ancient Mariner**

And now there came both mist and snow,
And it grew wondrous cold:
And ice, mast-high, some floating by,
As green as emerald.

And through the drifts the snowy cliffs
Did send a dismal sheen:
Nor shapes of men nor beasts we ken—
The ice was all between.

The ice was here, the ice was there,
The ice was all around:
It cracked and growled, and roared and howled,
Like noises in a swound.*

SAMUEL TAYLOR COLERIDGE

THE SNOW LIES SPRINKLED ON THE BEACH

The snow lies sprinkled on the beach,
And whitens all the marshy lea:
The sad gulls wail adown the gale,
The day is dark and black the sea.
   Shorn of their crests the blighted waves
With driven foam the offing fleck:

* *swoon; faint*

5

The ebb is low and barely laves
The red rust of the giant wreck.

On such a stony, breaking beach
My childhood chanced and chose to be:
'Twas here I played, and musing made
My friend the melancholy sea.
    He from his dim enchanted caves
With shuddering roar and onrush wild
Fell down in sacrificial waves
At feet of his exulting child.

Unto a spirit too light for fear
His wrath was mirth, his wail was glee:—
My heart is now too fixed to bow
Tho' all his tempests howl at me:
    For to the gain life's summer saves,
My solemn joy's increasing store,
The tossing of his mournful waves
Makes sweetest music evermore.

ROBERT BRIDGES

SEA LONGING

A thousand miles beyond this sun-steeped wall
    Somewhere the waves creep cool along the sand,
    The ebbing tide forsakes the listless land
With the old murmur, long and musical;
The windy waves mount up and curve and fall,
    And round the rocks the foam blows up like snow,—

6

Tho' I am inland far, I hear and know,
For I was born the sea's eternal thrall.
I would that I were there and over me
The cold insistence of the tide would roll,
Quenching this burning thing men call the soul,—
Then with the ebbing I should drift and be
Less than the smallest shell along the shoal,
Less than the seagulls calling to the sea.

SARA TEASDALE

SPRAY

It is a wonder foam is so beautiful.
A wave bursts in anger on a rock, broken up
in a wild white sibilant spray
and falls back, drawing in its breath with rage,
with frustration how beautiful!

D. H. LAWRENCE

MARINE

Waves that are white far out
Wear their way to the shore
Thunder running under.

The maned fall of the combers

Pours froth over, slowly,
Close in, and very shallow.

Waves that are white far out
Where the wind's will has its way
With water deep for sailing

Write long broken runes
In sand, for the poor student
To try construing over.

Waves that are white far out
Where treasure lies, deep down,
Fathoms below sounding,

Roll no richness here,
Only kelp to the margin,
Shell, or starfish, broken.

ROLFE HUMPHRIES

THE CATACLYSM

When a great wave disturbs the ocean cold
    And throws the bottom waters to the sky,
    Strange apparitions on the surface lie
Great battered vessels, stripped of gloss and gold,
And, writhing in their pain, sea-monsters old,
    Who stain the waters with a bloody dye,
    With unaccustomed mouths bellow and cry
And vex the waves with struggling fin and fold.

8

And with these too come little trivial things
   Tossed from the deep by the same casual hand;
   A faint sea flower, dragged from the lowest sand,
That will not undulate its luminous wings
In the slow tides again, lies dead and swings
   Along the muddy ripples to the land.

EDWARD SHANKS

SEA-SONNET

We have forgot, who safe in cities dwell,
The waters that a labouring planet bore;
Forgot to trace in their primeval lore
The shapeless epochs fluted to a shell.
Their old chaotic voices chronicle
The first confusion, and the dark, before
The first adventurer with spear and oar
Towards the unknown pushed out his coracle.*

Yet, to the requiem of a dying earth,
When man has passed, his fever and his pride,
Still shall the constellations find a grave
In that Pacific whence the moon had birth,
And that same moon shall heap the desolate tide
Beneath the night's unchanging architrave.**

V. SACKVILLE-WEST

* *a small boat*
** *round exterior of an arch*

9

THE EVEN SEA

Meekly the sea

now plods to shore:

white-faced cattle used to their yard,

the waves, with weary knees,

come back from bouldered hills

of high water,

where all the gray, rough day they seethed like bulls,

till the wind laid down its goads

at shift of tide, and sundown

gentled them; with lowered necks

they amble up the beach

as to their stalls.

MAY SWENSON

BY THE SALTINGS

When the wind is in the thrift
gently, down by the saltings,
at dawn when the vapours lift;

and pattering sanderlings*
run from you rather than fly
across the sandfist screaming;

before the runnels drain dry
among the sea-lavender
and sun severs sea from sky;

there is time enough, under
any listing low-tide hull
of your choosing, to wonder

at the force of it to pull
you to its shelter, alone
as you are and as fearful

as some crab beneath some stone.

                    TED WALKER

THE MAIN-DEEP

The long-rolling,
Steady-pouring,
Deep trenchèd
Green billow:

The wide-topped,
Unbroken,

* small shorebirds

11

Green-glacid,
Slow-sliding,

Cold-flushing,
—On—on—on—
Chill-rushing,
Hush-hushing,

. . . Hush—hushing. . . .

JAMES STEPHENS

A SEA SONG

In the days before the high tide
   Swept away the towers of sand
Built with so much labour
   By the children of the land,

Pale, upon the pallid beaches,
   Thirsting, on the thirsty sands,
Ever cried I to the Distance,
   Ever seaward spread my hands.

See, they come, they come, the ripples,
   Singing, singing fast and low,
Meet the longing of the sea-shores,
   Clasp them, kiss them once, and go.

"Stay, sweet Ocean, satisfying
    All desires into rest—"
Not a word the Ocean answered,
    Rolling sunward down the west.

Then I wept: "Oh who will give me
    To behold the stable sea,
On whose tideless shores for ever
    Sounds of many waters be?"

D. M. DOLBEN

WAVES

There's big waves and little waves,
    Green waves and blue,
Waves you can jump over,
    Waves you dive through,
Waves that rise up
    Like a great water wall,
Waves that swell softly
    And don't break at all,
Waves that can whisper,
    Waves that can roar,
And tiny waves that run at you
    Running on the shore.

ELEANOR FARJEON

ECHOES

The sea laments
The livelong day,
Fringing its waste of sand;
Cries back the wind from the whispering shore—
No words I understand:
Yet echoes in my heart a voice,
As far, as near, as these—
The wind that weeps,
The solemn surge
Of strange and lonely seas.

WALTER DE LA MARE

14

Fish
and Other
Creatures

O ye whales and all that move in the waters

—"Benedicite," THE BOOK OF COMMON PRAYER

from **PARADISE LOST**

And God said, let the Waters generate
Reptil with Spawn abundant, living Soule:
And let Fowle fli above the Earth, with wings
Displayed on th'op'n Firmament of Heav'n.
And God created the great Whales, and each
Soul living, each that crept, which plenteously
The waters generated by their kindes,
And every Bird of wing after his kinde;
And saw that it was good, and bless'd them, saying,
Be fruitful, multiply, and in the Seas
And Lakes and running Streams the waters fill;
And let the Fowle be multiply'd on the Earth.
Forthwith the Sounds and Seas, each Creek and Bay
With Frie innumerable swarme, and Shoales
Glide under the green Wave, in Sculles that oft
Bank. the mid Sea: part single or with mate
Graze the Sea weed thir pasture, and through Groves
Of Coral stray, or sporting with quick glance
Show to the Sun thir wav'd coats dropt with Gold,
Or in thir Pearlie shells at ease, attend
Moist nutriment, or under rocks thir food
In jointed Armour watch: on smooth the Seale
And bended Dolphins play: huge part of bulk
Wallowing unweildie, enormous in thir Gate
Tempest the Ocean: there Leviathan
Hugest of living Creatures, on the Deep
Stretcht like a Promontorie sleeps or swimmes,
And seems a moving Land, and at his Gilles
Draws in, and at his Trunck spouts out a Sea.

JOHN MILTON

TO FISH

You strange, astonish'd-looking, angle-faced,
  Dreary-mouth'd, gaping wretches of the sea,
  Gulping salt water everlastingly,
Cold-blooded, though with red your blood be graced,
And mute, though dwellers in the roaring waste;
  And you, all shapes beside, that fish be,—
  Some round, some flat, some long, all devilry,
Legless, unloving, infamously chaste:—

A scaly, slippery, wet, swift, staring wights,
  What is't ye do? What life lead? eh, dull goggles?
How do ye vary your vile days and nights?
  How pass your Sundays? Are ye still but joggles
In ceaseless wash? Still nought but gapes, and bites,
  And drinks, and stares, diversified with boggles?*

LEIGH HUNT

THE WHALE

At every stroke his brazen fins do take,
More circles in the broken sea they make
Than cannons' voices, when the air they tear:
His ribs are pillars, and his high arch'd roof
Of bark that blunts best steel, is thunder-proof:
Swim in him swallow'd dolphins, without fear,
And feel no sides, as if his vast womb were
Some inland sea, and ever as he went

* fumbles

17

He spouted rivers up, as if he meant
To join our seas with seas above the firmament.

He hunts not fish, but as an officer,
Stays in his court, at his own net, and there
All suitors of all sorts themselves enthrall;
So on his back lies this whale wantoning,
And in his gulf-like throat sucks everything
That passeth near. Fish chaseth fish, and all,
Flyer and follower, in this whirlpool fall;
O might not states of more equality
Consist? and is it of necessity
That thousand guiltless smalls, to make one great,
must die?

JOHN DONNE

WHALE

Rain, with a silver flail;
Sun, with a golden ball;
Ocean, wherein the whale
Swims minnow-small;
I heard the whale rejoice
And cynic sharks attend;
He cried with a purple voice,
"The Lord is my friend!"

"With flanged and battering tail,
With huge and dark baleen,*

* *whalebone*

18

He said, 'let there be whale
    In the Cold and Green!'

"He gave me a water spout,
    A side like a harbor wall;
The Lord from cloud looked out
    And planned it all.

"With glittering crown atilt
    He leaned on a glittering rail;
He said, 'Where sky is split,
    Let there be Whale.'

"Tier upon tier of wings
    Blushed and blanched and bowed;
Phalanxed fiery things
    Cried in the cloud;

"Million-eyed was the murk
    At the plan not understood;
But the Lord looked on His work
    And saw it was good.

"He gave me marvelous girth
    For the curve of back and breast,
And a tiny eye of mirth
    To hide His jest.

"He made me a floating hill,
    A plunging deep-sea mine.
This was the Lord's will;
    The Lord is divine.

"I magnify His name
  In earthquake and eclipse,
In weltering molten flame
  And wrecks of ships,

"In waves that lick the moon;
  I, the plough of the sea!
I am the Lord's boon,
  The Lord made me!"

The sharks barked from beneath,
  As the great whale rollicked and roared,
"Yes, and our grinning teeth,
  Was it not the Lord?"

Then question pattered like hail
  From fishes large and small.
"The Lord is mighty," said Whale,
  "The Lord made all!

"His is a mammoth jest
  Life never may betray;
He has laid it up in His breast
  Till Judgment Day;

"But high when combers foam
  And tower their last of all,
My power shall haul you home
  Through Heaven wall.

"A trumpet then in the gates,
  To the ramps a thundering drum,
I shall lead you where He waits,
  For His Whale to come.

"Where His cloudy seat is placed
    On high in an empty dome,
I shall trail the Ocean abased
    In chains of foam,

"Unwieldy, squattering dread;
    Where the blazing cohorts stand
At last I shall lift my head
    As it feels His hand.

"Then wings with a million eyes
    Before mine eyes shall quail:
'Look you, all Paradise,
    I was His Whale!' "

I heard the Whale rejoice,
    As he splayed the waves to a fan;
"And the Lord shall say with His Voice,
    'Leviathan!'

"The Lord shall say with His Tongue,
    'Now let all Heaven give hail
To my Jest when I was young,
    To my very Whale!' "

Then the Whale careered in the Sea,
    He floundered with flailing tail;
Flourished and rollicked he,
    "Aha! Mine Empery!
For the Lord said, 'Let Whale be!'
    And there was Whale!"

                    WILLIAM ROSE BENÉT

21

THE MALDIVE SHARK

About the shark, phlegmatical one,
Pale sot of the Maldive sea,
The sleek little pilot-fish, azure and slim,
How alert in attendance be.
From his saw-pit of mouth, from his charnel of maw
They have nothing of harm to dread,
But liquidly glide on his ghastly flank
Or before his Gorgonian head;
Or lurk in the port of serrated teeth
In white triple tiers of glittering gates,
And there find a haven when peril's abroad,
An asylum in jaws of the Fates!
They are friends; and friendly they guide him to prey,
Yet never partake of the treat—
Eyes and brains to the dotard lethargic and dull,
Pale ravener of horrible meat.

HERMAN MELVILLE

OVER THE GREEN SANDS

Leaning on the unpainted rail
We gazed into a fathom of water so clear
We were engulfed,
    And saw a darkness moving

Through the bottle green,
    A shadow creeping
Over the pale floor of tinted sand,
Coarse hair coiling and weaving—

Yet not a hair was displaced
It was an enormous school of miniature
    Fish who laced
The quiet flood with their immaculate coiffure.

Quivering up in precise formations,
The mannered swarm, cutting and hitching,
Threaded the water with live needles
    Which left no stitching.

We dropped our pebbles. The tiny darts
    Swerved wild.
Fluttering, badly mussed,
They hesitated for an instant.

    Then away they streaked,
Beside the stalks of wharves
Greenwigged with ferny gardens,
A sweep of mermaid hair.

Unburdened in defeat we watched
That neat, shy storm disappear
Over the green sands,
    Which are white in our world.

PEGGY BENNETT

THE HARPOONING

Where the seas are open moor
and level blue, limitless,
and swells are as soft grasses
rolling over with the wind,
often to the stillness
of Azorean summer

come the great whales. Long granites
grow, slowly awash with sun,
and waves lap long black skin
like the shine of a laving
rain upon a city pavement.
Together they come, yet alone

they seem to lie. Massively
still, they bask, breathing like men.
Silent among them there is one
so huge he enters the eye
whole, leaving the rest unseen.
His sons and his cows idly

loll as if in wait. Inside
him, too, tethered now, there waits
the bulk and strength of a herd
of a dozen rogue elephant;
they strain taut thongs of his will,
pawing against such indolence.

An anger could snap them loose—
anger or hunger. Jungles,

24

under a mile of ocean
where no light has ever been,
could splinter, and the blind squid
uncoil in him like oily trees.

But the squint jaws close on bone
steady as a castle doorjamb;
and, bigger than a drawbridge,
his tailflukes are calm upon
the calmer water. While the sun
still pleases him, he will grudge

himself no pleasure, He blows
old air from his old lungs, cones
rising whitely. Through the black
final coursings of warm blood
the oars will not rouse him. Thick
blubber houses him like hot meringue.

TED WALKER

SEAL

See how he dives
From the rocks with a zoom!
See how he darts
Through his watery room
Past crabs and eels
And green seaweed,
Past fluffs of sandy
Minnow feed!
See how he swims

With a swerve and a twist,
A flip of the flipper,
A flick of the wrist!
Quicksilver-quick,
Softer than spray,
Down he plunges
And sweeps away;
Before you can think,
Before you can utter
Words like "Dill pickle"
Or "Apple butter,"
Back up he swims
Past sting-ray and shark,
Out with a zoom,
A whoop, a bark;
Before you can say
Whatever you wish,
He plops at your side
With a mouthful of fish!

WILLIAM JAY SMITH

THE DANCING SEAL

When we were building Skua Light—
The first men who had lived a night
Upon that deep-sea Isle,
As soon as chisel touched the stone
The friendly seals would come ashore
And sit and watch us all the while,
As if they'd not seen men before,

And so, poor beasts, had never known
Men had the heart to do them harm.
They'd little cause to feel alarm
With us, for we were glad to find
Some friendliness in that strange sea,
Only too pleased to let them be
And sit as long as they'd a mind
To watch us, for their eyes were kind
Like women's eyes it seemed to me.
So hour on hour they sat: I think
They liked to hear the chisel's clink,
And when the boy sang loud and clear
They scrambled closer in to hear,
And if he whistled sweet and shrill
The queer beasts shuffled nearer still,
But every sleek and sheeny skin
Was mad to hear his violin.

When, work all over for the day,
He'd take his fiddle down and play
His merry tunes beside the sea,
Their eyes grew brighter and more bright
And burned and twinkled merrily;
And, as I watched them one still night
And saw their eager sparkling eyes,
I felt those lively seals would rise,
Some shiny night ere he could know,
And dance about him heel and toe
Unto the fiddle's heady tune.

And at the rising of the moon,
Half-daft, I took my stand before

A young seal lying on the shore
And called on her to dance with me:
And it seemed hardly strange when she
Stood up before me suddenly
And shed her black and sheeny skin
And smiled, all eager to begin . . .
And I was dancing heel and toe
With a young maiden white as snow
Unto a crazy violin.

We danced beneath the dancing moon
All night beside the dancing sea
With tripping toes and skipping heels,
And all about us friendly seals
Like Christian folk were dancing reels
Unto the fiddle's endless tune
That kept on spinning merrily
As though it never meant to stop;
And never once the snow-white maid
A moment stayed
To take a breath,
Though I was fit to drop;
And while those wild eyes challenged me
I knew as well as well could be
I must keep step with that young girl,
Though we should dance to death.

Then with a skirl
The fiddle broke:
The moon went out:
The sea stopped dead:
And in a twinkling all the rout

Of dancing folk had fled . . .
And in the chill bleak dawn I woke
Upon the naked rock alone.

They've brought me far from Skua Isle . . .
I laugh to think they do not know
That, as all day I chip the stone
Among my fellows here inland,
I smell the sea-wrack on the shore . . .
And see her snowy tossing hand,
And meet again her merry smile . . .
And dream I'm dancing all the while,
I'm dancing ever, heel and toe,
With a seal-maiden white as snow,
On that moonshiny island strand
For ever and for evermore.

WILFRED GIBSON

THE WHITE SEAL'S LULLABY

Oh! hush thee, my baby, the night is behind us,
    And black are the waters that sparkled so green.
The moon, o'er the combers, looks downward to find us
    At rest in the hollows that rustle between.
Where billow meets billow, then soft be thy pillow;
    Ah, weary wee flipperling, curl at thy ease!
The storm shall not wake thee, nor shark overtake thee,
    Asleep in the arms of the slow-swinging seas.

RUDYARD KIPLING

THE MOON-CHILD

A little lonely child am I
    That have not any soul:
God made me as the homeless wave,
    That has no goal.

A seal my father was, a seal
    That once was man:
My mother loved him tho' he was
    'Neath mortal ban.

He took a wave and drowned her,
    She took a wave and lifted him;
And I was born where shadows are
    In sea-depths dim.

All through the sunny blue-sweet hours
    I swim and glide in waters green:
Never by day the mournful shores
    By me are seen.

But when the gloom is on the wave
    A shell unto the shore I bring:
And then upon the rocks I sit
    And plaintive sing.

I have no playmate but the tide
    The seaweed loves with dark brown eyes:
The night-waves have the stars for play,
    For me but sighs.

WILLIAM SHARP

30

Sea Serpents

There is that leviathan whom thou has made to play therein.

—PSALM 104

THE HUGE LEVIATHAN

Toward the sea turning my troubled eye,
I saw the fish (if fish I may it cleep*)
That makes the sea before his face to fly,
And with his flaggy fins doth seem to sweep
The foamy waves out of the dreadful deep,
The huge Leviathan, dame Nature's wonder,
Making his sport, that many makes to weep:
A sword-fish small him from the rest did sunder,
That in his throat him pricking softly under,
His wide abyss him forced forth to spew,
That all the sea did roar like heaven's thunder,
And all the waves were stained with filthy hue.

EDMUND SPENSER

THE KRAKEN

Below the thunders of the upper deep;
Far, far beneath in the abysmal sea,
His ancient, dreamless, uninvaded sleep
The Kraken sleepeth: faintest sunlights flee
About his shadowy sides: above him swell
Huge sponges of millennial growth and height;
And far away into the sickly light,
From many a wondrous grot** and secret cell

* call
** grotto

32

Unnumber'd and enormous polypi
Winnow with giant arms the slumbering green.
There hath he lain for ages and will lie
Battening upon huge seaworms in his sleep,
Until the latter fire shall heat the deep;
Then once by man and angels to be seen,
In roaring he shall rise and on the surface die.

ALFRED, LORD TENNYSON

WATER-SNAKES
from **The Rime of the Ancient Mariner**

Beyond the shadow of the ship,
I watched the water-snakes:
They moved in tracks of shining white,
And when they reared, the elfish light
Fell off in hoary flakes.

Within the shadow of the ship
I watched their rich attire:
Blue, glossy green, and velvet black,
They coiled and swam; and every track
Was a flash of golden fire.

SAMUEL TAYLOR COLERIDGE

LEVIATHAN

Canst thou draw out leviathan with an hook? or his
    tongue with a cord thou lettest down?
Canst thou put an hook into his nose? or bore his jaw
    through with a thorn? . . .
Canst thou fill his skin with barbed irons? or his head
    with fish spears? . . .
Who can open the doors of his face? his teeth are terrible
    round about.
His scales are his pride, shut up together as with a close
    seal.
One is so near to another, that no air can come between
    them.
They are joined one to another, they stick together, that
    they cannot be sundered.
By his neesings* a light doth shine, and his eyes are like
    the eyelids of the morning.
Out of his mouth go burning lamps, and sparks of fire
    leap out.
Out of his nostrils goeth smoke, as out of a seething pot
    or cauldron.
His breath kindleth coals, and a flame goeth out of his
    mouth.
In his neck remaineth strength, and sorrow is turned
    into joy before him.
The flakes of his flesh are joined together; they are firm
    in themselves; they cannot be moved.
His heart is as firm as a stone; yea, as hard as a piece of
    the nether millstone.

* *sneezings*

34

When he raiseth up himself the mighty are afraid; by
    reason of breakings they purify themselves.
The sword of him that layeth at him cannot hold: the
    spear, the dart, nor the habergeon.*
He esteemeth iron as straw, and brass as rotten
    wood . . .
He maketh the deep to boil like a pot: he maketh the sea
    like a pot of ointment.
He maketh a path to shine after him; one would think
    the deep to be hoary.
Upon the earth there is not his like, who is made
    without fear.

THE BOOK OF JOB

LEVIATHAN

Leviathan drives the eyed prow of his face,
With the surge dumbly rippling round his lips,
Toward the Atlantid shore;
Not flat and golden like the Cherubim,
Or a face round and womanish like the Seraphim,
But thick and barbed—the broad, barbed cheeks of
    Donne.

Beneath he stretched his hands to the sea forests,
Obscure and thick, with the cool freshes under,
Lifts his surprised brows to the sky'd milky light,
New come from the abyss.

* *sleeveless coat of mail*

35

While a faint radiance, webbed from the waves'
    substance,
Clung to his changing limbs and his coiled body,
Reddening, making them darker than the sea,
Or half translucent.

And when the mouths of Atlantean brooks
Struck on his mouth with taste of sudden cold
And wound his shoulders like embracing hands,
He put out both thick palms and felt the shallows.

The salt had scurfed his body with white fire
And knotted the rough hair between his breasts,
And as he rose delicate Atlantis trembled,
Tilting upon the sea's plain like a leaf.

The passionless air hung heavy on Atlantis,
And the inclined spears of the flowering bushes
Smoothly dropped down their loosened, threaded petals,
Softening the pathways.

For tideless night had covered her, and sealed
All scent within the narrow throat of flowers,
And sound within the navel of the hills,
And stars in the confusion of the air.

Within her darkness and unconsciousness
She hid all beauty, and her silences
Sounds measurers and sequences,
And the black earth quickened
With oppression of blossom.

Ah, thief that swims by night—Leviathan,
Rolled blindly in the wave's trough like a rotting thing,
Come to Atlantis' further edge by dark,
Poised over her quietness;

Measureless drunkard of the bitter sea,
Insatiate, like some slow stain
Creeping on pleasure's face,
Like sudden misery.

So foul, so desolate,
That you are crept to seek new life,
Having crossed the water's plain,
Desiring and by stealth to gain
For rankness, foolishness and half-conceivèd beauty
Some perfect shape—an Atlantean body.

PETER QUENNELL

THE SEA WOLF

The fishermen say, when your catch is done
    And you're sculling in with the tide,
You must take great care that the Sea Wolf's share
    Is tossed to him overside.

They say that the Sea Wolf rides, by day,
    Unseen on the crested waves,
And the sea mists rise from his cold green eyes
    When he comes from his salt sea caves.

The fishermen say, when it storms at night
   And the great seas bellow and roar,
That the Sea Wolf rides on the plunging tides,
   And you hear his howl at the door.

And you must throw open your door at once,
   And fling your catch to the waves,
Till he drags his share to his cold sea lair,
   Straight down to his salt sea caves.

Then the storm will pass, and the still stars shine,
   In peace—so the fishermen say—
But the Sea Wolf waits by the cold Sea Gates
   For the dawn of another day.

VIOLET MC DOUGAL

Birds
of the Ocean
and Shore

Goneys an' gullies an' all o' the birds o' the sea

—JOHN MASEFIELD

THE STORMY PETREL

A thousand miles from land are we,
Tossing about on the roaring sea,—
From billow to bounding billow cast,
Like fleecy snow on the stormy blast.
The sails are scattered abroad like weeds;
The strong masts shake like quivering reeds;
The mighty cables and iron chains,
The hull, which all earthly strength disdains,—
They strain and they crack; and hearts like stone
Their natural, hard, proud strength disown.

Up and down!—up and down!
From the base of the waves to the billows crown,
And amidst the flashing and feathery foam
The stormy petrel finds a home,—
A home, if such a place may be
For her who lives on the wide, wide sea,
On the craggy ice, in the frozen air,
And only seeketh her rocky lair
To warm her young, and to teach them to spring
At once o'er the waves on their stormy wing!

O'er the deep!—o'er the deep!
Where the whale and the shark and the swordfish
    sleep,—
Outflying the blast and the driving rain,
The petrel telleth her tale—in vain;
For the mariner curseth the warning bird
Which bringeth him news of the storm unheard!
Ah! thus does the prophet, of good or ill,

Meet hate from the creatures he serveth still;
Yet he ne'er falters,—so, petrel, spring
Once more o'er the waves on thy stormy wing!

BRYAN WALLER PROCTER

SEA-BIRDS

O lonesome sea-gull, floating far
    Over the ocean's icy waste,
Aimless and wide thy wanderings are,
    Forever vainly seeking rest:—
    Where is thy mate, and where thy nest?

'Twixt wintry sea and wintry sky,
    Cleaving the clean air with thy breast,
Thou sailest slowly, solemnly;
    No fetter on thy wing is pressed:—
    Where is thy mate, and where thy nest?

O restless, homeless human soul,
    Following for aye* thy nameless quest,
The gulls float, and the billows roll;
    Thou watchest still, and questionest:—
    Where is *thy* mate, and where thy nest?

ELIZABETH AKERS

* *ever*

HERRING-GULL

Run seaward, launch upon the air, and sound your
    desolate cry
Over these shores and waters; the wind on which you
    rest
Air-borne, as sea-borne on the ocean's undulant breast,
Buoys you on, hunting the waste with hungry eye.

Are there, beyond these crowded shores, beyond your
    call
And waiting your return to their sandy bed,
Young, ravenous beaks strained skyward, gaping to be
    fed?
A need is on you, a great need is on us all.

Balance upon the wind, send out your desolate cry
To the four corners of the waste, your clamor is
The clamor of life in bondage to the old necessities—
Torment that is the thrust of some immortal joy.

JOHN HALL WHEELOCK

THE STORM

First there were two of us, then there were three of us,
Then there was one bird more,
Four of us—wild white sea-birds,
Treading the ocean floor;
And the *wind* rose, and the *sea* rose,
To the angry billows' roar—

42

With one of us—two of us—three of us—four of us
Sea-birds on the shore.

Soon there were five of us, soon there were nine of us,
And lo! in a trice sixteen!
And the yeasty surf curdled over the sands,
The gaunt grey rocks between;
And the tempest raved, and the lightning's fire
Struck blue on the spindrift* hoar—
And on four of us—ay, and on four times four of us
Sea-birds on the shore.

And our sixteen waxed to thirty-two,
And they to past three score—
A wild, white welter of winnowing wings,
And ever more and more;
And the winds lulled, and the sea went down,
And the sun streamed out on high,
Gilding the pools and the spume and the spars
'Neath the vast blue deeps of the sky;

And the isles and the bright green headlands shone,
As they'd never shone before,
Mountains and valleys of silver cloud,
Wherein to swing, sweep, soar—
A host of screeching, scolding, scrabbling
Sea-birds on the shore—
A snowy, silent, sun-washed drift
Of sea-birds on the shore.

WALTER DE LA MARE

* spray

43

SEAGULLS ON THE SERPENTINE

Memory, out of the mist, in a long slow ripple
    Breaks, blindly, against the shore.
The mist has buried the town in its own oblivion.
    This, this is the sea once more.

Mist—mist—brown mist; but a sense in the air of snow-
     flakes!
    I stand where the ripples die,
Lift up an arm and wait, till my lost ones know me,
    Wheel overhead, and cry.

Salt in the eyes, and the seagulls, mewing and
     swooping,
    Snatching the bread from my hand;
Brushing my hand with their breasts, in swift caresses
    To show that they understand.

Oh, why are you so afraid? We are all of us exiles!
    Wheel back in your clamorous rings!
We have all of us lost the sea, and we all remember.
    But you—have wings.

ALFRED NOYES

AFTERNOON: AMAGANSETT BEACH

    The broad beach,
Sea-wind and the sea's irregular rhythm,
Great dunes with their pale grass, and on the beach

Driftwood, tangle of bones, an occasional shell,
Now coarse, now carven and delicate—whorls of time
Stranded in space, deaf ears listening
To lost time, old oceanic secrets.
Along the water's edge, in pattern casual
As the pattern of the stars, the pin-point air-holes,
Left by the sand-flea under the receding spume,
Wink and blink out again. A gull drifts over,
Wide wings crucified against the sky—
His shadow travels the shore, upon its margins
You will find his signature: one long line,
Two shorter lines curving out from it, a neatly
Perfect graph of the bird himself in flight.
His footprint is his image fallen from heaven.

JOHN HALL WHEELOCK

GREEN SHAG*

On the wave-washed scarp of crag
Broods the haggard hungry shag
Over the green curdling sea,
Like some ancient huddled hag
Gloating o'er the witchery
Of her seething cauldron, brewing
Hell-broth for a king's undoing.

WILFRED GIBSON

* cormorant: a sea bird

45

BIRDS

The fierce musical cries of a couple of sparrow hawks
     hunting on the headland,
Hovering and darting, their heads northwestward,
                    Prick like silver arrows shot
     through a curtain the noise of the ocean
Trampling its granite; their red backs gleam
Under my window around the stone corners; nothing
     gracefuller, nothing
Nimbler in the winds. Westward the wave-gleaners,
The old gray sea-going gulls are gathered together, the
     northwest wind wakening
Their wings to the wild spirals of the wind-dance.
Fresh as the air, salt as the foam, play birds in the bright
     wind, fly falcons
Forgetting the oak and the pinewood, come gulls
From the Carmel sands and the sands at the river-mouth,
     from Lobos and out of the limitless
Power of the mass of the sea, for a poem
Needs multitude, multitudes of thoughts, all fierce, all
     flesh-eaters, musically clamorous
Bright hawks that hover and dart headlong, and
     ungainly
Gray hungers fledged with desire of transgression, salt
     slimed beaks, from the sharp
Rock-shores of the world and the secret waters.

ROBINSON JEFFERS

46

SKIMMERS

Where you see the undersides of their wings
the whole mass is white and flickering in the sunlight
above the sandbar and the blue water of the sound
and you can hear them crying and protesting
in the cool sea wind that blows across the channel

and where the rest of them are turning toward you
they are all black and flickering in the sunlight
and they go swinging in a long Cartesian figure
like a twisted plane that lets you see its outlines
by its colors, the one half white and tilting away,

and the other half black and tilting toward you,
as they swing into the air and call you all the names
they can think of in the time it takes to rise
and get away, loping on their long black wings
so leisurely toward the sound behind the islands.

PAUL BAKER NEWMAN

from A CANTICLE TO THE WATERBIRDS

Clack your beaks you cormorants and kittiwakes,
North on those rackcroppings fingerjutted into the rough
    Pacific surge;
You migratory terns and pipers who leave but the
    temporal claw-track written on sandbars there of
    your presence;

Grebes and pelicans; you comber-picking scoters and
    you long-shore gulls;
All you keepers of the coastline north of here to the
    Mendocino beaches;
All you beyond the cliff-face thwarting the surf at Hecate
    Head,
Hovering the under-surge where the cold Columbia
    grapples at the bar;
North yet to the Sound, whose islands float like a sown
    flurry of chips upon the sea:
Break wide your harsh and salt-encrusted beaks unmade
    for song
And say a praise up to the Lord.

BROTHER ANTONINUS

SEA-HAWK

The six-foot nest of the sea-hawk,
Almost inaccessible,
Surveys from the headland the lonely, the violent waters.

I have driven him off,
Somewhat foolhardily,
And look into the fierce eye of the offspring.

It is an eye of fire,
An eye of icy crystal,
A threat of ancient purity,

Power of an immense reserve,
An agate-well of purpose,
Life before man, and maybe after.

How many centuries of sight
In this piercing, inhuman perfection
Stretch the gaze off the rocky promontory,

To make the mind exult
At the eye of a sea-hawk,
A blaze of grandeur, permanence of the impersonal.

RICHARD EBERHART

TO THE MAN-OF-WAR BIRD

Thou who hast slept all night upon the storm,
Waking renew'd on thy prodigious pinions,
(Burst the wild storm? Above it thou ascended'st
And rested on the sky, thy slave that cradled thee),
Now a blue point, far, far in heaven floating,
As to the light emerging here on deck I watch thee,
(Myself a speck, a point on the world's floating vast.)

Far, far at sea,
After the night's fierce drifts have strewn the shore with
      wrecks,
With re-appearing day as now so happy and serene,
The rosy and elastic dawn, the flashing sun,
The limpid spread of air cerulean,
Thou also re-appearest.

Thou born to match the gale, (thou art all wings)
To cope with heaven and earth and sea and hurricane,
Thou ship of air that never furl'st thy sails
Days, even weeks untired and onward, through spaces,
    realms,
At dusk that look'st on Senegal, at morn America,
That sport'st amid the lightning-flash and thunder-
    cloud,
In them, in thy experiences, had'st thou my soul,
What joys! what joys were thine!

WALT WHITMAN

THE ECHOING CLIFF

White gulls that sit and float
Each on his shadow like a boat,
Sandpipers, oystercatchers
And herons, those grey stilted watchers,
From loch* and corran** rise,
And as they scream and squawk abuse
Echo from wooded cliff replies
So clearly that the dark pine boughs,
Where goldcrests flit
And owls in drowsy wisdom sit,
Are filled with sea-birds and their cries.

ANDREW YOUNG

lake
**bay*

50

THE CURLEW

A curlew, scouting for his flock,
Came on me suddenly as I
Sat staring at the sea and sky,
And perched upon a rock

Not twenty paces from my hand.
And since I did not stir or speak,
He smoothed his feathers with his beak
And skipped along the sand,

And with a bright, unstartled eye
Observed the stranger on his beach,
Then made a little chattering speech
And teetered delicately

Upon his reedy legs. Unknown
Although my status was, his guess
Was that I had some business
With Sea, or were a stone

Unswayed by any winds that blow
From what dark wastes of north or east,
Solid and sure and safe—at least
He judged me to be so.

SARA HENDERSON HAY

THE SANDPIPER

Across the narrow beach we flit,
    One little sandpiper and I,
And fast I gather, bit by bit,
    The scattered driftwood bleached and dry.
The wild waves reach their hands for it,
    The wild wind raves, the tide runs high,
As up and down the beach we flit,—
    One little sandpiper and I.

Above our heads the sullen clouds
    Scud black and swift across the sky;
Like silent ghosts in misty shrouds
    Stand out the white lighthouses high.
Almost as far as eye can reach
    I see the close-reefed vessels fly,
As fast we flit along the beach,—
    One little sandpiper and I.

I watch him as he skims along,
    Uttering his sweet and mournful cry.
He starts not at my fitful song,
    Or flash of fluttering drapery.
He has no thought of any wrong;
    He scans me with a fearless eye:
Staunch friends are we, well tried and strong,
    The little sandpiper and I.

Comrade, where wilt thou be tonight
    When the loosed storm breaks furiously?
My driftwood fire will burn so bright!
    To what warm shelter canst thou fly?

I do not fear for thee, though wroth
    The tempest rushes through the sky:
For are we not God's children both,
    Thou, little sandpiper, and I.

CELIA THAXTER

THE SANDPIPER

Along the sea-edge, like a gnome
Or rolling pebble in the foam,
As though he timed the ocean's throbbing,
Runs a piper, bobbing, bobbing.

Now he stiffens, now he wilts,
Like a little boy on stilts!
Creatures burrow, insects hide,
When they see the piper glide.

You would think him out of joint,
Till his bill begins to point.
You would doubt if he could fly,
Till his straightness arrows by.

You would take him for a clown,
Till he peeps and flutters down,
Vigilant among the grasses,
Where a fledgling bobs and passes.

WITTER BYNNER

Shells

*Gather a shell from the strown beach
And listen at its lips*

—DANTE GABRIEL ROSSETTI

SCARLETT ROCKS

I thought of life, the outer and the inner,
    As I was walking by the sea:
How vague, unshapen this, and that, though thinner,
    Yet hard and clear in its rigidity.
Then took I up the fragment of a shell,
    And saw its accurate loveliness,
And searched its filmy lines, its pearly cell,
    And all that keen contention to express
A finite thought. And then I recognised
    God's working in the shell from root to rim,
And said: 'He works till He has realised—
    O Heaven! if I could only work like Him!'

T. E. BROWN

from **THE EXCURSION**

                    I have seen
A curious child, who dwelt upon a tract
Of inland ground, applying to his ear
The convolutions of a smooth-lipped shell;
To which, in silence hushed, his very soul
Listened intensely; and his countenance soon
Brightened with joy; for from within were heard
Murmurings, whereby the monitor expressed
Mysterious union with its native sea.

WILLIAM WORDSWORTH

from **GEBIR**

    I have sinuous shells of pearly hue
Within, and they that lustre have imbibed
In the sun's palace porch; where when unyoked
His chariot wheel stands midway in the wave.
Shake one, and it awakens, then apply
Its polished lips to your attentive ear,
And it remembers its august abodes,
And murmurs as the ocean murmurs there.

WALTER SAVAGE LANDOR

THE SHELL

I

See what a lovely shell,
Small and pure as a pearl,
Lying close to my foot,
Frail, but a work divine,
Made so fairily well
With delicate spire and whorl,
How exquisitely minute,
A miracle of design!

II

What is it? a learned man
Could give it a clumsy name.
Let him name it who can,
The beauty would be the same.

III

The tiny shell is forlorn,
Void of the little living will
That made it stir on the shore.
Did he stand at the diamond door
Of his house in a rainbow frill?
Did he push, when he was uncurled,
A golden foot or a fairy horn
Through his dim water-world?

IV

Slight, to be crushed with a tap
Of my finger-nail on the sand,
Small, but a work divine,
Frail, but of force to withstand,
Year upon year, the shock
Of cataract seas that snap
The three-decker's oaken spine
Athwart the ledges of rock,
Here on the Breton strand!

ALFRED, LORD TENNYSON

FRUTTA DI MARE*

I am a sea-shell flung
Up from the ancient sea;
Now I lie here, among
Roots of a tamarisk tree;
No one listens to me.

I sing to myself all day
In a husky voice, quite low,

* *Fruits of the Sea*

Things the great fishes say
And you most need to know;
All night I sing just so.

But lift me from the ground,
And hearken at my rim,
Only your sorrow's sound,
Amazed, perplexed and dim,
Comes coiling to the brim;

For what the wise whales ponder
Awaking from sleep,
The key to all your wonder,
The answers of the deep,
These to myself I keep.

GEOFFREY SCOTT

THE SHELL

And then I pressed the shell
Close to my ear,
And listened well.

And straightway, like a bell,
Came low and clear
The slow, sad murmur of far distant seas,

Whipped by an icy breeze
Upon a shore

Wind-swept and desolate.

It was a sunless strand that never bore
The footprint of a man,
Nor felt the weight

Since time began
Of any human quality or stir,
Save what the dreary winds and waves incur.

And in the hush of waters was the sound
Of pebbles, rolling round;
For ever rolling, with a hollow sound:

And bubbling sea-weeds, as the waters go,
Swish to and fro
Their long cold tentacles of slimy grey;

There was no day;
Nor ever came a night
Setting the stars alight

To wonder at the moon:
Was twilight only, and the frightened croon,
Smitten to whimpers, of the dreary wind

And waves that journeyed blind . . .
And then I loosed my ear—O, it was sweet
To hear a cart go jolting down the street!

JAMES STEPHENS

61

THE SEA-LIMITS

Consider the sea's listless chime:
  Time's self it is, made audible,—
  The murmur of the earth's own shell.
Secret continuance sublime
  Is the sea's end: our sight may pass
  No furlong further. Since time was,
This sound hath told the lapse of time.

No quiet, which is death's,—it hath
  The mournfulness of ancient life,
  Enduring always at dull strife.
As the world's heart of rest and wrath,
  Its painful pulse is in the sands.
  Last utterly, the whole sky stands,
Grey and not known, along its paths.

Listen alone beside the sea,
  Listen alone among the woods;
  Those voices of twin solitudes
Shall have one sound alike to thee:
  Hark where the murmurs of thronged men
  Surge and sink back and surge again,—
Till the one voice of wave and tree.

Gather a shell from the strown beach
  And listen at its lips: they sigh
  The same desire and mystery,
The echo of the whole sea's speech.
  And all mankind is thus at heart

Not anything but what thou art:
And Earth, Sea, Man, are all in each.

DANTE GABRIEL ROSSETTI

THE SHELL

What has the sea swept up?
A Viking oar, long mouldered in the peace
Of grey oblivion? Some dim-burning bowl
Of unmixed gold, from far-off island feasts?
Ropes of old pearls? Masses of ambergris?
Something of elfdom from the ghastly isles
Where white-hot rocks pierce through the flying
      spindrift?*
Or a pale sea-queen, close wound in a net of spells?

Nothing of these. Nothing of antique splendours
That have a weariness about their names:
But—fresh and new, in frail transparency,
Pink as a baby's nail, silky and veined
As a flower petal—this casket of the sea,
One shell.

MARY WEBB

* spray

THE CHAMBERED NAUTILUS

This is the ship of pearl, which, poets feign,
    Sails the unshadowed main,—
    The venturous bark that flings
On the sweet summer wind its purpled wings
In gulfs enchanted, where the Siren sings,
    And coral reefs lie bare,
Where the cold sea-maids rise to sun their streaming
    hair.

Its webs of living gauze no more unfurl;
    Wrecked is the ship of pearl!
    And every chambered cell,
Where its dim dreaming life was wont to dwell,
As the frail tenant shaped his growing shell,
    Before thee lies revealed,—
Its irised ceiling rent, its sunless crypt unsealed!

Year after year beheld the silent toil
    That spread his lustrous coil;
    Still, as the spiral grew,
He left the past year's dwelling for the new,
Stole with soft step its shining archway through,
    Built up its idle door,
Stretched in his last-found home, and knew the old no
    more.

Thanks for the heavenly message brought by thee,
    Child of the wandering sea,
    Cast from her lap, forlorn!
From thy dead lips a clearer note is born

Than ever Triton blew from wreathèd horn!
  While on mine ear it rings,
Through the deep caves of thought I hear a voice that
    sings:—

Build thee more stately mansions, O my soul,
  As the swift seasons roll!
  Leave thy low-vaulted past!
Let each new temple, nobler than the last,
Shut thee from heaven with a dome more vast,
  Till thou at length are free,
Leaving thine outgrown shell by life's unresting sea!

                    OLIVER WENDELL HOLMES

THE SHELL

Who could devise
But the dark sea this thing
Of depth, of dyes
Claws of weeds cling,
Whose colour cries:
'I am of water, as of air the wing',
Yet holds the eyes
As though they looked on music perishing?

Yet the shell knows
Only its own dark chamber
Coiled in repose
Where without number
One by one goes

Each blind wave, feeling mother-of-pearl and amber,
Flooding, to close
A book all men might clasp, yet none remember.

Too far away
For thought to find the track,
Sparkling with spray
Rose, green and black,
The colours play,
Strained by the ebb, revealing in the wrack
The myth of day,
A girl too still to call her bridegroom back.

There falls the weight
Of glory unpossessed;
There the sands late
Hold the new guest
Whose ponderous freight
Draws the pool's hollow like a footprint pressed.
Its outcast state
Suddenly seems miraculous and blest.

Turn it; now hold
Its ancient heart. How fair
With lost tales told
In sea-salt air
Light's leaf-of-gold
Leaps from the threshold up the spiral stair,
Then lost, is cold,
Bound in a flash to rock with Ariadne's hair.

VERNON WATKINS

66

ECSTASY

I saw a frieze on whitest marble drawn
Of boys who sought for shells along the shore,
Their white feet shedding pallor in the sea,
The shallow sea, the spring-time sea of green
That faintly creamed against the cold, smooth
     pebbles. . . .

One held a shell unto his shell-like ear
And there was music carven in his face.
His eyes half-closed, his lips just breaking open
To catch the lulling, mazy, coralline roar
Of numberless caverns filled with singing seas.

And all of them were hearkening as to singing
Of far-off voices thin and delicate,
Voices too fine for any mortal wind
To blow into the whorls of mortal ears—
And yet those sounds flowed from their grave, sweet
     faces.

And as I looked I heard that delicate music,
And I became as grave, as calm, as still
As those carved boys. I stood upon that shore,
I felt the cool sea dream around my feet,
My eyes were staring at the far horizon. . . .

WALTER J. TURNER

67

ON SOME SHELLS FOUND INLAND

These are my murmur-laden shells that keep
A fresh voice tho' the years lie very gray.
The wave that washed their lips and tuned their lay
Is gone, gone with the faded ocean sweep,
The royal tide, gray ebb and sunken neap
And purple midday,—gone! To this hot clay
Must sing my shells, where yet the primal day,
Its roar and rhythm and splendour will not sleep.
What hand shall join them to their proper sea
If all be gone? Shall they forever feel
Glories undone and worlds that cannot be?—
'T were mercy to stamp out this agèd wrong,
Dash them to earth and crunch them with the heel
And make a dust of their seraphic song.

TRUMBULL STICKNEY

from EACH AND ALL

The delicate shells lay on the shore;
The bubbles of the latest wave
Fresh pearls to their enamel gave,
And the bellowing of the savage sea
Greeted their safe escape to me.
I wiped away the weeds and foam,
I fetched my sea-born treasures home;
But the poor, unsightly, noisome things
Had left their beauty on the shore
With the sun and the sand and the wild uproar.

RALPH WALDO EMERSON

Seaweed, Anemones and Coral

*The sea blooms and the oozy woods which wear
The sapless foliage of the ocean*

—P. B. SHELLEY

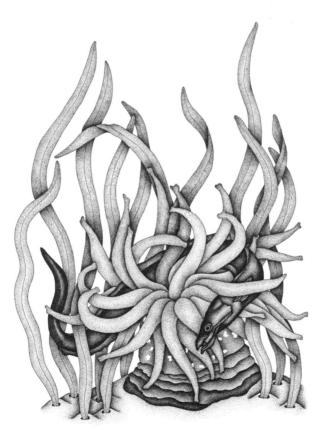

A SEALESS WORLD

There shall be no more sea

If when I come to Paradise
The Lord do not provide
The salt tang of seaweed
And the running of the tide,
And if as the book saith
There shall be no more sea,
Then all the peace of Paradise
Shall not comfort me.

If when I come to Paradise
The Lord do not provide
Pools fringed and sea pinks
And ribbed sands stretching wide,
If no gulls call shrilly
Across a ruffled sea,
Then all the songs of Paradise
Shall *not* solace me.

JOAN CAMPBELL

THE SEA RITUAL

Prayer unsaid, and mass unsung,
Deadman's dirge must still be rung:
  Dingle-dong, the dead-bells sound!
  Mermen chant his dirge around!

Wash him bloodless, smoothe him fair,
Stretch his limbs, and sleek his hair:
  Dingle-dong, the dead-bells go!
  Mermen swing them to and fro!

In the wormless sands shall he
Feast for no foul gluttons be:
  Dingle-dong, the dead-bells chime!
  Mermen keep the tune and time!

We must with a tombstone brave
Shut the shark from out his grave:
  Dingle-dong, the dead bells toll!
  Mermen's dirgers ring his knoll!

Such a slab will we lay o'er him
All the dead shall rise before him!
  Dingle-dong, the dead-bells boom!
  Mermen lay him in his tomb!

GEORGE DARLEY

from **THE TEMPEST**

Full fathom five thy father lies;
   Of his bones are coral made;
Those are pearls that were his eyes:
   Nothing of him that doth fade,
But doth suffer a sea-change
Into something rich and strange.
Sea-nymphs hourly ring his knell:
                   Ding-dong.
   Hark! now I hear them—
   Ding-dong, bell!

WILLIAM SHAKESPEARE

D'AVALOS' PRAYER

When the last sea is sailed and the last shallow charted,
   When the last field is reaped and the last harvest
     stored,
When the last fire is out and the last guest departed,
   Grant the last prayer that I shall pray, Be good to me,
     O Lord!

And let me pass in a night at sea, a night of storm and
     thunder,
   In the loud crying of the wind through sail and rope
     and spar;

Send me a ninth great peaceful wave to drown and roll
　　me under
　　　To the cold tunny-fishes* home where the drowned
　　　galleons are.

And in the dim green quiet place far out of sight and
　　hearing,
　　　Grant I may hear at whiles** the wash and thresh of
　　　the sea-foam
About the fine keen bows of the stately clippers steering
　　Toward the lone northern star and the fair ports of
　　home.

JOHN MASEFIELD

CARDIGAN BAY

Clean, green, windy billows notching out the sky,
Grey clouds tattered into rags, sea-winds blowing high,
And the ships under topsails, beating, thrashing by,
　　And the mewing of the herring gulls.

Dancing, flashing green seas shaking white locks,
Boiling in blind eddies over hidden rocks,
And the wind in the rigging, the creaking of the blocks,
　　And the straining of the timber hulls.

* *tuna*
** *at times*

73

Delicate, cool sea-weeds, green and amber-brown,
In beds where shaken sunlight slowly filters down
On many a drowned seventy-four,* and many a sunken
   town,
   And the whitening of the dead men's skulls.

JOHN MASEFIELD

from **KING RICHARD III**

Lord, lord! methought what pain it was to drown;
What dreadful noise of water in mine ears!
What sights of ugly death within mine eyes!
Methought I saw a thousand fearful wracks;**
A thousand men that fishes gnaw'd upon;
Wedges of gold, great anchors, heaps of pearl,
Inestimable stones, unvalu'd jewels,
All scattered in the bottom of the sea.
Some lay in dead men's skulls; and in those holes
Where eyes did once inhabit, there were crept
As 'twere in scorn of eyes, reflecting gems,
That woo'd the slimy bottom on the deep,
And mocked the dead bones that lay scatter'd by.

WILLIAM SHAKESPEARE

* *warship with 74 guns*
** *wrecks*

THE WORLD BELOW THE BRINE

The world below the brine;
Forests at the bottom of the sea—the branches and
    leaves,
Sea lettuce, vast lichens, strange flowers and seeds—the
    thick tangle, the openings, and the pink turf,
Different colors, pale gray and green, purple, white and
    gold—the play of light through the water,
Dumb swimmers there among the rocks—coral, gluten,
    grass, rushes—and the aliment of the swimmers,
Sluggish existences grazing there, suspended, or slowly
    crawling close to the bottom,
The sperm whale at the surface, blowing air and spray,
    or disporting with his flukes,
The leaden-eyed shark, the walrus, the turtle, the hairy
    sea leopard, and the sting ray;
Passions there—wars, pursuits, tribes—sight in those
    ocean depths—breathing that thick-breathing air,
    as so many do;
The change thence to the sight here, and to the subtle air
    breathed by beings like us, who walk this sphere;
The change onward from ours, to that of beings who
    walk other spheres.

WALT WHITMAN

SEA-WEED

Sea-weed sways and sways and swirls
as if swaying were its form of stillness;
and if it flushes against fierce rock
it slips over it as shadows do, without hurting itself.

D. H. LAWRENCE

from LOOK NOT TOO DEEP

Sleeplessly circle the waves
Far under, and dumbly resound
In throats of the sea-filled caves,
Where daylight wholly is drowned,
Where frail fair shells are scattered
And broken in random foam,
With weeds that have found no home,
And drift-wood of ships long shattered.

LAURENCE BINYON

BY THE SEA

Why does the sea moan evermore?
    Shut out from heaven it makes its moan,

It frets against the boundary shore;
  All earth's full rivers cannot fill
  The sea, that drinking thirsteth still.

Sheer miracles of loveliness
  Lie hid in its unlooked-on bed:
Anemones, salt passionless,
  Blow flower-like; just enough alive
  To blow and multiply and thrive.

Shells quaint with curve, or spot, or spike,
  Encrusted live things argus-eyed,*
All fair alike, yet all unlike,
  Are born without a pang, and die
  Without a pang, and so pass by.

CHRISTINA ROSSETTI

SEAWEED

When descends on the Atlantic
  The gigantic
Storm-wind of the equinox,
Landward in his wrath he scourges
  The toiling surges,
Laden with seaweed from the rocks:

* Argus—a figure in Greek mythology, had 100 eyes

77

From Bermuda's reefs; from edges
    Of sunken ledges,
In some far-off, bright Azore;
From Baham, and the dashing,
    Silver-flashing
Surges of San Salvador;

From the tumbling surf, that buries
    The Orkneyan skerries,
Answering the hoarse Hebrides;
And from wrecks of ships, and drifting
    Spars, uplifting
On the desolate, rainy seas;—

Ever drifting, drifting, drifting
    On the shifting
Currents of the restless main;
Till in sheltered coves, and reaches
    Of sandy beaches,
All have found repose again.

HENRY WADSWORTH LONGFELLOW

THE ROCK POOL

Bright as a fallen fragment of the sky,
    'Mid shell-encrusted rocks the sea-pool shone,
Glassing the sunset-clouds in its clear heart,
A small enchanted world enwalled apart
        In diamond mystery,

Content with its own dreams, its own strict zone
    Of urchin woods, its fairy bights* and bars,
    Its daisy-disked anemones and rose-feathered stars.

Forsaken for awhile by that deep roar
    Which works in storm and calm the eternal will,
Drags down the cliffs, bids the great hills go by
And shepherds their multitudinous pageantry,—
        Here, on this ebb-tide shore
A jewelled bath of beauty, sparkling still,
    The little sea-pool smiled away the sea,
    And slept on its own plane of bright tranquility.

A self-sufficing soul, a pool in trance,
    Un-stirred by all the spirit winds that blow
From o'er the gulfs of change, content, ere yet
On its own crags, which rough peaked limpets fret
        The last rich colours glance,
Content to mirror the sea-birds' wings of snow,
    Or feel in some small creek, ere sunset fails,
    A tiny Nautilus hoist its lovely purple sails;

And, furrowing into pearl that rosy bar,
    Sail its own soul from fairy fringe to fringe,
Lured by the twinkling prey 'twas born to reach
In its own pool, by many an elfin beach
        Of jewels, adventuring far
Through the last mirrored cloud and sunset-tinge
    And past the rainbow-dripping cave where lies
    The dark green pirate-crab with beaded eyes,

* *coves*

Or fringed Medusa floats like light in light,
      Medusa, with the loveliest of all fays*
Pent in its irised bubble of jellied sheen,
Trailing long ferns of moonlight, shot with green
            And crimson rays and white,
Waving ethereal tendrils, ghostly sprays,
      Daring the deep, dissolving in the sun,
      The vanishing point of life, the light whence life
      begun.

ALFRED NOYES

TIDAL POOL

Here at the turning of the tide,
The sea swung in against the shore,
And drew a long, slow breath, and tried
Again, and gained a cranny more.

Its fingers probed the ledges, bare,
Dry in the alien sun, and then
Withdrew, but the small creatures there
Under the kelp took heart again.

* fairies

80

Feeling their element flow back,
The little world of pools became
Suddenly animate; the slack
Ribbons of weed rose up like flame

And wavered on the watery floor.
The mussel, from his pearly house,
Peered out; the snail unlatched his door,
Righted himself, began to browse

Along his pasturage of rock.
The shrimp, in arched and flimsy mail,
Went skittering backward, and a flock
Of spiders skated under sail.

I, leaning from my point of air,
Could almost, by a sleight of mind,
Become a size with them and share
A world, a universe defined

By smaller boundaries, but which bore
Like mine, such purpose and such pride,
As if they both were something more
Than a brief interval of tide.

SARA HENDERSON HAY

THE ROCK POOL

This is the sea. In these uneven walls
    A wave lies prisoned. Far and far away
Outward to ocean, as the slow tide falls,
    Her sisters through the capes that hold the bay
Dancing in lovely liberty recede.
    Yet lovely in captivity she lies,
Filled with soft colours, where the wavering weed
    Moves gently and discloses to our eyes
Blurred shining veins of rock and lucent shells
    Under the light-shot water; and here repose
Small quiet fish and dimly glowing bells
    Of sleeping sea-anemones that close
Their tender fronds and will not now awake
Till on these rocks the waves returning break.

EDWARD SHANKS

THE CORAL GROVE

Deep in the wave is a coral grove,
Where the purple mullet and gold-fish rove;
Where the sea-flower spreads its leaves of blue
That never are wet with falling dew,
But in bright and changeful beauty shine
Far down in the green and glassy brine.
The floor is of sand, like the mountain drift,

And the pearl-shells spangle the flinty snow;
From coral rocks the sea-plants lift
Their boughs, where the tides and billows flow:
The water is calm and still below,
For the winds and waves are absent there,
And the sands are bright as the stars that glow
In the motionless fields of upper air.
There, with its waving blade of green,
The sea-flag streams through the silent water,
And the crimson leaf of the dulse is seen
To blush, like a banner bathed in slaughter.
There, with a light and easy motion,
The fan-coral sweeps through the clear deep sea;
And the yellow and scarlet tufts of ocean
Are bending like corn on the upland lea:
And life, in rare and beautiful forms,
Is sporting amid those bowers of stone,
And is safe when the wrathful Spirit of storms
Has made the top of the wave his own.
And when the ship from his fury flies,
Where the myriad voices of Ocean roar;
When the wind-god frowns in the murky skies,
And demons are waiting the wreck on shore;
Then, far below, in the peaceful sea,
The purple mullet and gold-fish rove,
Where the waters murmur tranquilly,
Through the bending twigs of the coral grove.

JAMES GATES PERCIVAL

THE POOL IN THE ROCK

In this water, clear as air,
Lurks a lobster in its lair.
Rock-bound weed sway out and in,
Coral-red and bottle-green.
Wondrous pale anemones
Stir like flowers in a breeze:
Fluted scallop, whelk in shell,
And the prowling mackerel.
Winged with snow the sea-mews ride
The brine-keen wind; and far and wide
Sounds on the hollow thunder of the tide.

WALTER DE LA MARE

from **THE BOROUGH**

Now is it pleasant in the summer-eve,
When a broad shore retiring waters leave,
Awhile to wait upon the firm fair sand,
When all is calm at sea, all still at land;
And there the ocean's produce to explore,
As floating by, or rolling on the shore;
Those living jellies which the flesh inflame,
Fierce as a nettle, and from that its name;
Some in huge masses, some that you may bring
In the small compass of a lady's ring;

84

Figured by hand divine—there's not a gem
Wrought by man's art to be compared with them;
Soft, brilliant, tender, through the wave they glow,
And make the moonbeams brighter where they flow.
Involved in sea-wrack, here you find a race,
Which science, doubting, knows not where to place;
On shell or stone is dropp'd the embryo-seed,
And quickly vegetates a vital breed.

While thus with pleasing wonder you inspect
Treasures the vulgar in their scorn reject,
See as they float along th'entangled weeds
Slowly approach, upborne on bladdery beads;
Wait till they land, and you shall then behold
The fiery sparks those tangled fronds infold,
Myriads of living points; th'unaided eye
Can but the fire and not the form descry.
And now your view upon the ocean turn,
And there the splendour of the waves discern;
Cast but a stone, or strike them with an oar,
And you shall flames within the deep explore;
Or scoop the stream phosphoric* as you stand,
And the cold flames shall flash along your hand;
When, lost in wonder, you shall walk and gaze
On weeds that sparkle, and on waves that blaze.

GEORGE CRABBE

* *phosphorescent*

Sunken Cities

Land-under-wave . . . out of the moon's light and the sun's

—W. B. YEATS

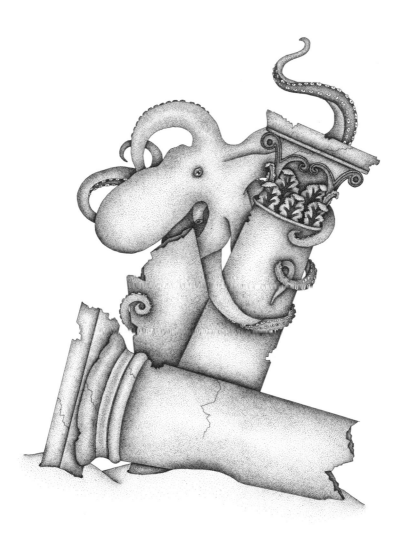

ATLANTIS

There was an island in the sea
That out of immortal chaos reared
Towers of topaz, trees of pearl,
For maidens adored and warriors feared.

Long ago it sunk in the sea;
And now, a thousand fathoms deep,
Sea-worms above it whirl their lamps,
Crabs on the pale mosaic creep.

Voyagers over that haunted sea
Hear from the waters under the keel
A sound that is not wave or foam;
Nor do they only hear, but feel

The timbers quiver, as eerily comes
Up from the dark an elfin singing
Of voices happy as none can be,
And bells an ethereal anthem ringing.

Thereafter, where they go or come,
They will be silent; they have heard
Out of the infinite of the soul
An incommunicable word;

Thereafter, they are as lovers who
Over an infinite brightness lean:
'It is Atlantis!', all their speech;
'To lost Atlantis have we been.'

CONRAD AIKEN

FRAGMENTS

In some green island of the sea,
    Where now the shadowy coral grows
In pride and pomp and empery
    The courts of old Atlantis rose.

In many a glittering house of glass
    The Atlanteans wandered there;
The paleness of their faces was
    Like ivory, so pale they were.

And hushed they were, no noise of words
    In those bright cities ever rang;
Only their thoughts, like golden birds,
    About their chambers thrilled and rang.

*   *   *

The green and greedy seas have drowned
    That city's glittering walls and towers,
Her sunken minarets are crowned
    With red and russet water-flowers.

In towers and rooms and golden courts
    The shadowy coral lifts her sprays;
The scrawl hath gorged her broken orts,*
    The shark doth haunt her hidden ways.

But, at the falling of the tide,
    The golden birds still sing and gleam,

* *scraps*

89

The Atlanteans have not died,
Immortal things still give us dream.

JOHN MASEFIELD

from THE DYING PATRIOT

Evening on the olden, the golden sea of Wales,
When the first star shivers and the last wave pales:
O evening dreams!
There's a house that Britons walked in, long ago,
Where now the springs of ocean fall and flow,
And the dead robed in red and sea-lilies overhead
Sway when the long winds blow.

JAMES ELROY FLECKER

CITIES DROWNED

Cities drowned in olden time
Keep, they say, a magic chime
Rolling up from far below
When the moon-led waters flow.

So within me, ocean deep,
Lies a sunken world asleep.

Lest its bells forget to ring,
Memory! Set the tide a-swing!

HENRY NEWBOLT

SUNK LYONESSE

In sea-cold Lyonesse,
When the Sabbath eve shafts down
On the roofs, walls, belfries
Of the foundered town,
The Nereids pluck their lyres
Where the green translucency beats,
And with motionless eye at gaze
Make minstrelsy in the streets.

And the ocean water stirs
In salt-worn casemate and porch.
Plies the blunt-snouted fish
With fire in his skull for torch.
And the ringing wires resound;
And the unearthly lovely weep,
In lament of the music they make
In the sullen courts of sleep:
Whose marble flowers bloom for aye:
And—lapped by the moon-guiled tide—
Mock their carver with heart of stone,
Caged in his stone-ribbed side.

WALTER DE LA MARE

THE CITY IN THE SEA

Lo! Death has reared himself a throne
In a strange city lying alone
Far down within the dim West,
Where the good and the bad and the worst and the best
Have gone to their eternal rest.
There shrines and palaces and towers
(Time-eaten towers that tremble not!)
Resemble nothing that is ours.
Around, by lifting winds forgot,
Resigned, beneath the sky
The melancholy waters lie.

No rays from the holy heaven come down
On the long night-time of that town;
But light from out the lurid sea
Streams up the turrets silently—
Gleams up the pinnacles far and free—
Up domes—up spires—up kingly halls—

Up fanes*—up Babylon-like walls—
Up shadowy long-forgotten bowers
Of sculptured ivy and stone flowers—
Up many and many a marvellous shrine
Whose wreathed friezes intertwine
The viol, the violet, and the vine.

Resignedly beneath the sky
The melancholy waters lie.

* *temples*

So blend the turret and shadows there
That all seem pendulous in air,
While from a proud tower in the town
Death looks gigantically down.

There open fanes and gaping graves
Yawn level with the luminous waves;
But not the riches there that lie
In each idol's diamond eye—
Not the gaily-jewelled dead
Tempt the waters from their bed;
For no ripples curl, alas!
Along that wilderness of glass—
No swellings tell that winds may be
Upon some far-off happier sea—
No heavings hint that winds have been
On seas less hideously serene.

But lo, a stir is in the air!
The wave—there is a movement there!
As if the towers had thrust aside,
In slightly sinking, the dull tide—
As if their tops had feebly given
A void within the filmy Heaven.
The waves now have a redder glow—
The hours are breathing faint and low—
And when, amid no earthly moans,
Down, down that town shall settle hence,
Hell, rising from a thousand thrones,
Shall do it reverence.

EDGAR ALLAN POE

Mermaids and Mermen

Teach me to hear mermaids singing

—JOHN DONNE

THE SEA-FAIRIES

Slow sail'd the weary mariners and saw,
Betwixt the green brink and the running foam,
Sweet faces, rounded arms, and bosoms prest
To little harps of gold; and while they mused
Whispering to each other half in fear,
Shrill music reach'd them on the middle sea.

Whither away, whither away, whither away? fly no
    more.
Whither away from the high green field, and the happy
    blossoming shore?
Day and night to the billow the fountain calls:
Down shower the gambolling waterfalls
From wandering over the lea:
Out of the live-green heart of the dells
They freshen the silvery-crimson shells,
And thick with white bells the clover-hill swells
High over the full-toned sea:
O hither, come hither and furl your sails,
Come hither to me and to me:
Hither, come hither and frolic and play;
Here it is only the mew* that wails;
We will sing to you all the day:
Mariner, mariner, furl your sails,
For here are the blissful downs and dales,
And merrily, merrily carol the gales,
And the spangle dances in bight and bay,
And the rainbow forms and flies on the land
Over the islands free;

* *gull*

96

Hither, come hither and see;
And the rainbow hangs on the poising wave,
And sweet is the colour of cove and cave,
And sweet shall your welcome be:
O hither, come hither, and be our lords,
For merry brides are we:
We will kiss sweet kisses, and speak sweet words:
O listen, listen, your eyes shall glisten
When the sharp clear twang of the golden chords
Runs up the ridged sea.
Who can light on as happy a shore
All the world o'er, all the world o'er?
Whither away? listen and stay: mariner, fly no more.

ALFRED, LORD TENNYSON

THE MERMAID

I

Who would be
A mermaid fair,
Singing alone,
Combing her hair
Under the sea,
In a golden curl
With a comb of pearl,
On a throne?

II

I would be a mermaid fair;
I would sing to myself the whole of the day;

With a comb of pearl I would comb my hair;
And still as I combed I would sing and say,
"Who is it loves me? who loves not me?"
I would comb my hair till my ringlets would fall
　　Low adown, low adown,
From under my starry sea-bud crown
　　Low adown and around,
And I should look like a fountain of gold
　　Springing alone
　　With a shrill inner sound,
　　Over the throne
　　In the midst of the hall;
Till that great sea-snake under the sea
From his coiled sleeps in the central deeps
Would slowly trail himself sevenfold
Round the hall where I sate,* and look in at the gate
With his large calm eyes for the love of me.
And all the mermen under the sea
Would feel their immortality
Die in their hearts for the love of me.

III

But at night I would wander away, away,
　　I would fling on each side my low-flowing locks,
And lightly vault from the throne and play
　　With the mermen in and out of the rocks;
We would run to and fro, and hide and seek,
　　On the broad sea-wolds** in the crimson shells,
　　Whose silvery spikes are nighest the sea.

* sat
** open uncultivated country

But if any came near I would call, and shriek,
And adown the steep like a wave I would leap
    From the diamond-ledges that jut from the dells;
For I would not be kissed by all who would list,
Of the bold merry mermen under the sea;
They would sue me, and woo me, and flatter me,
In the purple twilights under the sea;
But the king of them all would carry me,
Woo me, and win me, and marry me,
In the branching jaspers under the sea;
Then all the dry pied things that be
In the hueless mosses under the sea
Would curl round my silver feet silently,
All looking up for the love of me.
And if I should carol aloud, from aloft
All things that are forked, and horned, and soft
Would lean out from the hollow sphere of the sea,
All looking down for the love of me.

ALFRED, LORD TENNYSON

THE MERMAN

I

Who would be
A merman bold,
Sitting alone,
Singing alone
Under the sea,
With a crown of gold,
On a throne?

II

I would be a merman bold,
I would sit and sing the whole of the day;
I would fill the sea-halls with a voice of power;
But at night I would roam abroad and play
With the mermaids in and out of the rocks,
Dressing their hair with the white sea-flower;
And holding them back by their flowing locks
I would kiss them often under the sea,
And kiss them again till they kissed me,
       Laughingly, laughingly;
And then we would wander away, away
To the pale-green sea-groves straight and high,
       Chasing each other merrily.

III

There would be neither moon nor star;
But the wave would make music above us afar—
Low thunder and light in the magic light—
       Neither moon nor star.
We would call aloud in the dreamy dells,
Call to each other and whoop and cry
       All night merrily, merrily:
They would pelt me with starry spangles and shells,
Laughing and clapping their hands between,
       All night, merrily, merrily:
But I would throw to them back in mine
Turkis* and agate and almondine:**

* *turquoise*
** *garnet*

Then leaping out upon them unseen
I would kiss them often under the sea,
And kiss them again till they kissed me
        Laughingly, laughingly.
Oh! what a happy life were mine
Under the hollow-hung ocean green!
Soft are the moss-beds under the sea;
We would live merrily, merrily.

ALFRED, LORD TENNYSON

MERMAIDS

Leagues, leagues over
The sea I sail
Couched on a wallowing
Dolphin's tail:
The sky is on fire
The waves a-sheen;
I dabble my foot
In the billows green.

In a sea-weed hat
On the rocks I sit
Where tern and sea-mew
Glide and beat,
Where dark as shadows
The cormorants meet.

In caverns cool
When the tide's a-wash,
I sound my conch
To the watery splash.

From out their grottoes
At evening's beam
The mermaids swim
With locks agleam

To where I watch
On the yellow sands;
And they pluck sweet music
With sea-cold hands.

They bring me coral
And amber clear;
But when the stars
In heaven appear
Their music ceases,
They glide away,
And swim to their grottoes
Across the bay.

Then listen only
To my shrill tune
The surfy tide,
And the wandering moon.

WALTER DE LA MARE

from THE VISION OF THE MERMAIDS

Mermaids six or seven,
Ris'n from the deeps to gaze on sun and heaven,
Cluster'd in troops and halo'd by the light,
Those Cyclads made that thicken'd on my sight.
This was their manner: one translucent crest
Of tremulous film, more subtle than the vest
Of dewy gorse blurr'd with the gossamer fine,
From crown to tail-fin floating, fringed the spine,
Droop'd o'er the brows like Hector's casque, and sway'd
In silken undulation, spurr'd and ray'd
With spiked quills all of intensest hue;
And was as tho' some sapphire molten-blue
Were vein'd and streak'd with dusk-deep lazuli,
Or tender pinks with bloody Tyrian dye.
From their white waists a silver skirt was spread
To mantle o'er the tail, such as is shed
Around the Water-Nymphs in fretted falls,
At red Pompeii on medallion'd walls.
A tinted fin on either shoulder hung:
Their pansy-dark or bronzen locks were strung
With coral, shells, thick-pearled cords, whate'er
The abysmal Ocean hoards of strange and rare.

GERARD MANLEY HOPKINS

103

THE MERMAID

A mermaid found a swimming lad,
Picked him for her own,
Pressed her body to his body,
Laughed; and plunging down
Forgot in cruel happiness
That even lovers drown.

WILLIAM BUTLER YEATS

from A MIDSUMMER NIGHT'S DREAM

My gentle Puck, come hither. Thou rememberest
Since once I sat upon a promontory,
And heard a mermaid, on a dolphin's back,
Uttering such dulcet and harmonious breath,
That the rude sea grew civil at her song,
And certain stars shot madly from their spheres,
To hear the sea-maid's music.

WILLIAM SHAKESPEARE

KENNACK SANDS

On Kennack Sands the sun
Shines, and the fresh wind blows,

Moulding pale banks anew,
Where the sea-holly grows.
Waters softly blue
And exquisitely clear
Meet the o'er-arching sky;
O'er them the breezes run.
There may'st thou idly lie,
And still find new delights,
Watching the gulls' white flights
Above that lonely place;
Listen, nor ever hear
A single human sound
To spoil the free, profound,
Aerial quietness.
But when thou'rt gone, the night
On Kennack comes; and soon,
Lovely beyond dreams,
Arises the round moon;
In whose trembling light
The rough splendour gleams
Of the crested sea.
Ah, could'st thou there then be!
But mortal ears can hear not
What those pale sands hear then;
Sounds not of mortal birth,
Laughter, and dance, and mirth,
Of the golden-haired sea-fairies,
Mermaidens and mermen.

LAURENCE BINYON

THE FORSAKEN MERMAN

Come, dear children, let us away;
Down and away below.
Now my brothers call from the bay;
Now the great winds shorewards blow;
Now the salt tides seawards flow;
Now the wild white horses play,
Champ and chafe and toss in the spray.
Children dear, let us away.
This way, this way.

Call her once before you go,
Call once yet.
In a voice that she will know:
'Margaret! Margaret!'
Children's voices should be dear
(Call once more) to a mother's ear:
Children's voices, wild with pain.
Surely she will come again.
Call her once and come away.
This way, this way.
'Mother dear, we cannot stay.'
The wild white horses foam and fret.
Margaret! Margaret!

Come, dear children, come away down.
Call no more.
One last look at the white-wall'd town,
And the little grey church on the windy shore.
Then come down.

She will not come though you call all day,
Come away, come away.

Children dear, was it yesterday
We heard the sweet bells over the bay?
In the caverns where we lay,
Through the surf and through the swell,
The far-off sound of a silver bell?
Sand-strewn caverns, cool and deep,
Where the winds are all asleep;
Where the spent lights quiver and gleam;
Where the salt weed sways in the stream;
Where the sea-beasts rang'd all round
Feed in the ooze of their pasture ground;
Where the sea-snakes coil and twine,
Dry their mail and bask in the brine;
Where great whales come sailing by,
Sail and sail with unshut eye,
Round the world for ever and aye?*
When did music come this way?
Children dear, was it yesterday?

Children dear, was it yesterday
(Call yet once) that she went away?
Once she sate with you and me,
On a red gold throne in the heart of the sea,
And the youngest sate on her knee.
She comb'd its bright hair, and she tended it well,
When down swung the sound of the far-off bell.
She sigh'd, she look'd up through the clear green sea.

* ever

She said; 'I must go, for my kinsfolk pray
In the little grey church on the shore to-day.
'Twill be Easter-time in the world—ah me!
And I lose my poor soul, Merman, here with thee.'
I said; 'Go up, dear heart, through the waves;
Say thy prayer, and come back to the kind sea-caves.'
She smil'd, she went up through the surf in the bay.
Children dear, was it yesterday?

  Children dear, were we long alone?
'The sea grows stormy, the little ones moan.
Long prayers,' I said, 'in the world they say.
Come,' I said, and we rose through the surf in the bay.
We went up the beach, by the sandy down
Where the sea-stocks bloom, to the white-wall'd town.
Through the narrow pav'd streets, where all was still,
To the little grey church on the windy hill.
From the church came a murmur of folk at their prayers,
But we stood without in the cold blowing airs.
We climb'd on the graves, on the stones, worn with
      rains,
And we gaz'd up the aisle through the small leaded
      panes.
She sate by the pillar; we saw her clear;
'Margaret, hist! come quick, we are here.
Dear heart,' I said, 'we are long alone.
The sea grows stormy, the little ones moan.'
But, ah, she gave me never a look,
For her eyes were seal'd to the holy book.
Loud prays the priest; shut stands the door.
Come away, children, call no more.
Come away, come down, call no more.

Down, down, down.
Down to the depths of the sea.
She sits at her wheel in the humming town,
Singing most joyfully.
Hark, what she sings; 'O joy, O joy,
For the humming street, and the child with its toy.
For the priest, and the bell, and the holy well.
For the wheel where I spun,
And the blessed light of the sun.'
And so she sings her fill,
Singing most joyfully,
Till the shuttle falls from her hand,
And the whizzing wheel stands still.
She steals to the window, and looks at the sand;
And over the sand at the sea;
And her eyes are set in a stare;
And anon there breaks a sigh;
And anon there drops a tear,
From a sorrow-clouded eye,
And a heart sorrow-laden,
A long, long sigh,
For the cold strange eyes of a little Mermaiden,
And the gleam of her golden hair.

Come away, away children.
Come children, come down.
The hoarse wind blows colder;
Lights shine in the town.
She will start from her slumber
When gusts shake the door;
She will hear the winds howling,
Will hear the waves roar.

We shall see, while above us
The waves roar and whirl,
A ceiling of amber,
A pavement of pearl.
Singing, 'Here came a mortal,
But faithless was she.
And alone dwell for ever
The kings of the sea.'

But, children, at midnight,
When soft the winds blow;
When clear falls the moonlight;
When spring-tides are low;
When sweet airs come seaward
From heaths starr'd with broom;*
And high rocks throw mildly
On the blanch'd sands a gloom;
Up the still, glistening beaches,
Up the creeks we will hie;
Over banks of bright seaweed
The ebb-tide leaves dry.
We will gaze, from the sand-hills,
At the white, sleeping town;
At the church on the hill-side—
    And then come back down.
Singing, 'There dwells a lov'd one,
But cruel is she.
She left lonely for ever
The kings of the sea.'

MATTHEW ARNOLD

* low shrub with yellow flowers

Neptune and His Court

Hear old Triton blow his wreathèd horn.

—WILLIAM WORDSWORTH

IN PRAISE OF NEPTUNE

Of Neptune's empire let us sing,
At whose command the waves obey;
To whom the rivers tribute pay,
Down the high mountains sliding;
To whom the scaly nation yields
Homage for the crystal fields
    Wherein they dwell;
And every sea-god pays a gem
Yearly out of his watery cell,
To deck great Neptune's diadem.

The Tritons dancing in a ring,
Before his palace gates do make
The water with their echo quake,
Like the great thunder sounding:
The sea-nymphs chant their accents shrill,
And the Sirens taught to kill
    With their sweet voice,
Make every echoing rock reply,
Unto their gentle murmuring noise,
The praise of Neptune's empery.

THOMAS CAMPION

SONG BY LADY HAPPY, AS A SEA-GODDESS

My cabinets are oyster-shells,
In which I keep my Orient pearls:
And modest coral I do wear,
Which blushes when it touches air.

On silver waves I sit and sing,
And then the fish lie listening:
Then resting on a rocky stone
I comb my hair with fish's bone:

The whilst Apollo with his beams
Doth dry my hair from soaking streams,
His light doth glaze the water's face,
And make the sea my looking glass.

So when I swim on waters high,
I see myself as I glide by,
But when the sun begins to burn,
I back into my waters turn,

And dive unto the water low:
Then on my head the waters flow
In curled waves in circles round,
And thus with eddies I am crowned.

M. CAVENDISH, DUCHESS OF
NEWCASTLE

from A FRAGMENT

I have heard a voice of broken seas
And from the cliffs a cry.
Ah still they learn, those cave-eared Cyclades,
The Triton's friendly or his fearful horn,
And why the deep sea-bells but seldom chime,
And how those waves and with what spell-swept rhyme
In years of morning, on a summer's morn
Whispering round his castle on the coast,
Lured young Achilles from his haunted sleep
And drave* him out to dive beyond those deep
Dim purple windows of the empty swell,
His ivory body flitting like a ghost
Over the holes where flat blind fishes dwell
All to embrace his mother thronèd in her shell.

JAMES ELROY FLECKER

NEPTUNE
from **Comus**

Neptune, besides the sway
Of every salt flood and each ebbing stream,
Took in, by lot 'twixt high and nether Jove,
Imperial rule of all the sea-girt isles
That, like to rich and various gems, inlay
The unadornèd bosom of the deep;

---

* *drove*

114

Which he, to grace his tributary gods,
By course commits to several government,
And gives them leave to wear their sapphire crowns
And wield their little tridents.

NEPTUNE

As Pluto ruled the underworld
In shadowed majesty,
And Jupiter the overworld,
Neptune ruled the sea.

His cavalcade across the waves
Was marvellous to view;
His Tritons through the windy caves
Of conches music blew;

Great sea-horses his chariot swept
From oceans chill and grey
To purple seas where dolphins leapt
In showers of rainbow spray;

From pearly shells his Nereids peered,
Old Neptune's laughing girls;
His four winds blew his sea-green beard
Into a million curls;

His breakers, tall as emerald towers
With turrets white as milk,

Sank smooth as meadows strewn with flowers,
And left a sea like silk.

Where sun a golden road did blaze,
And moon a silver made:
Thus upon the ocean-ways
Rolled Neptune's cavalcade.

ELEANOR FARJEON

SONG
from **Comus**

Sabrina fair,
    Listen where thou art sitting
Under the glassy, cool, translucent wave,
    In twisted braids of lilies knitting
The loose train of thy amber-dropping hair;
    Listen for dear honour's sake,
    Goddess of the silver lake,
        Listen and save!

Listen, and appear to us,
In name of great Oceanus,
By the earth-shaking Neptune's mace,
And Tethys' grave majestic pace;
By hoary Nereus' wrinkled look,
And the Carpathian wizard's hook;
By scaly Triton's winding shell,
And old soothsaying Glaucus' spell;
By Leucothea's lovely hands,

And her son that rules the strands;
By Thetis' tinsel-slippered feet,
And the song of Sirens sweet;
By dead Parthenope's dear tomb,
And fair Ligea's golden comb,
Wherewith she sits on diamond rocks
Sleeking her soft alluring locks;
By all the nymphs that nightly dance
Upon thy streams with wily glance;
Rise, rise, and heave thy rosy head
From thy coral-paven* bed,
And bridle in thy headlong wave,
Till thou our summons answered have.
                    Listen and save!

                              JOHN MILTON

* *paved*

Swimmers

And in the water's soft caress,
Wash the mind of foolishness.

—RUPERT BROOKE

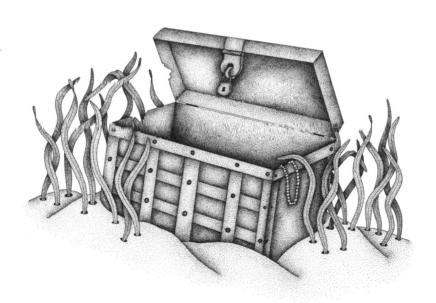

from A SWIMMER'S DREAM

A dream, a dream is it all—the season,
    The sky, the water, the wind, the shore?
A day-born dream of living unreason,
    A marvel moulded of sleep—no more?
For the cloud-like wave that my limbs while cleaving
Feel as in slumber beneath them heaving
Soothes the sense as to slumber, leaving
    Sense of nought that was known of yore.

A purer passion, a lordlier leisure,
    A peace more happy than lives on land,
Fulfils with pulse of diviner pleasure
    The dreaming head and the steering hand.
I lean my cheek to the cold grey pillow,
The deep soft swell of the full broad billow,
And close mine eyes for delight past measure,
    And wish the wheel of the world would stand.

The wild-winged hour that we fain would capture
    Falls as from heaven that its light feet clomb,
So brief, so soft, and so full of rapture
    Was felt that soothed me with sense of home.
To sleep, to swim, and to dream, for ever—
Such joy the vision of man saw never;
For here too soon will a dark day sever
    The sea-bird's wing from the sea-wave's foam.

A dream, and more than a dream, and dimmer
    At once and brighter than dreams that flee,
The moment's joy of the seaward swimmer

Abides, remembered as truth may be.
Not all the joy and not all the glory
Must fade as leaves when the woods wax hoary;
For there the downs and the sea-banks glimmer,
And here to south of them swells the sea.

ALGERNON CHARLES SWINBURNE

from THE ENCHANTED ISLAND

Some would dive in the lagoon
Like sunbeams, and all round our isle
Swim thro' the lovely crescent moon,
Glimpsing, for breathless mile on mile,
The wild sea-woods that bloomed below,
The rainbow fish, the coral cave
Where vanishing swift as melting snow
A mermaid's arm would wave.

Then dashing shoreward thro' the spray
On sun-lit seas they cast them down,
Or in the white sea-daisies lay
With sun-stained bodies rosy brown,
Content to watch the foam-bows flee
Across the shelving reefs and bars,
With wild eyes gazing out to sea
Like happy haunted stars.

ALFRED NOYES

SEA-CHANGE

Wind-flicked and ruddy her young body glowed
In sunny shallows, splashing them to spray;
But when on rippled silver sand she lay,
And over her the little green waves flowed,
Coldly translucent and moon-coloured showed
Her frail young beauty, as if rapt away
From all the light and laughter of the day
To some twilit, forlorn sea-god's abode.

Again into the sun with happy cry
She leapt alive and sparkling from the sea,
Sprinkling white spray against the hot blue sky,
A laughing girl . . . and yet I see her lie
Under a deeper tide eternally
In cold moon-coloured immortality.

WILFRED GIBSON

THE ICE-CART

Perched on my city office stool
I watched with envy while a cool
And lucky carter handled ice . . .
And I was wandering in a trice
Far from the grey and grimy heat
Of that intolerable street
O'er sapphire berg and emerald floe
Beneath the still cold ruby glow
Of everlasting Polar night,

Bewildered by the queer half-light,
Until I stumbled unawares
Upon a creek where big white bears
Plunged headlong down with flourished heels
And floundered after shining seals
Through shivering seas of blinding blue.
And as I watched them, ere I knew
I'd stripped and I was swimming too
Among the seal-pack, young and hale,
And thrusting on with threshing tail,
With twist and twirl and sudden leap
Through crackling ice and salty deep,
Diving and doubling with my kind
Until at last we left behind
Those big white blundering bulks of death,
And lay at last with panting breath
Upon a far untravelled floe
Beneath a gentle drift of snow—
Snow drifting gently fine and white
Out of the endless Polar night,
Falling and falling evermore
Upon that far untravelled shore
Till I was buried fathoms deep
Beneath that cold white drifting sleep
Sleep drifting deep,
Deep drifting sleep. . . .

The carter cracked a sudden whip:
I clutched my stool with startled grip,
Awakening to the grimy heat
Of that intolerable street.

WILFRED GIBSON

123

DIVER

Diver go down
Down through the green
Inverted dawn
To the dark unseen
To the never day
The under night
Starless and steep
Deep beneath deep
Diver fall
And falling fight
Your weed-dense way
Until you crawl
Until you touch
Weird water land
And stand.

Diver come up
Up through the green
Into the light
The sun   the seen
But in the clutch
Of your dripping hand
Diver bring
Some uncouth thing
That we could swear
And would have sworn
Was never born

Or could ever be
Anywhere
Blaze on our sight
Make us see.

ROBERT FRANCIS

THE LOVELY SWIMMERS

Diving for wrecks or sunken treasure, see
them, or for spoil, or delight and sweet ease
of the skin: boy, girl: silently
carving the deep underseas

illuminated fluid and color-change:
see them double, turn in a rapture
of quiet and pure form, arrange
by flight and pensive pursuit their capture

of motion in water: see them, purged
by immersion in liquid calms, pursue
the upper light and, with dark heads emerged,
decorate, those lovely swimmers, the bright blue.

RICHMOND LATTIMORE

MOON-BATHERS

Falls from her heaven the Moon, and stars sink burning
Into the sea where blackness rims the sea,
Silently quenched. Faint light that the waves hold
Is only light remaining; yet still gleam
The sands where those now-sleeping young moon-
    bathers
Came dripping out of the sea and from their arms
Shook flakes of light, dancing on the foamy edge
Of quiet waves. They were all things of light
Tossed from the sea to dance under the Moon—
Her nuns, dancing within her dying round,
Clear limbs and breasts silvered with Moon and waves
And quick with windlike mood and body's joy,
Withdrawn from alien vows, by wave and wind
Lightly absolved and lightly all forgetting.
    An hour ago they left. Remains the gleam
Of their late motion on the salt sea-meadow,
As loveliest hues linger when the sun's gone
And float in the heavens and die in reedy pools—
So slowly, who shall say when light is gone?

JOHN FREEMAN

THE DIVERS

Ah, look,
How sucking their last sweetness from the air
These divers run upon the pale sea verge;

An evening air so smooth my hand could round
And grope a circle of the hollow sky
Without a harshness or impediment.

Look now,
How they run cowering and each unknots
A rag, a girdle twisted on his loins,
Stands naked, quivered in the cool of night.

As boldest lovers will tire presently,
When dawn dries up a radiance on the limbs,
And lapse to common sleep,
To the deep tumult of habitual dreams,
Each sighing, with loosened limbs, as if regretfully,
Gives up his body to the foamless surge.

Water combs out his body, and he sinks
Beyond all form and sound.
Only the blood frets on,
Grown fearful, in a shallow dissonance.

Water strains on his hair and drums upon his flank,
Consumes his curious track
And straight or sinuous path
Dissolves as swift, impermanent as light.

Still his strange purpose drives him, like a beam,
Like the suspended shaft of cavern-piercing sun;
And, hardier still,
With wavering hands divides the massive gloom,—
A vast caress through which he penetrates,
Or obscure death withdrawing

Veil upon veil,
Discovering new darkness and profounder terror.

'Consider you your loss,
For now what strength of foot or hand
Can take you by the narrow way you came
Through the clear darkness up again and up.
Watch a procession of the living days,
Where dawn and evening melt so soft together
As wine in water, or milk shed in water,
Flaming and clouding into even dullness.'

'Who weeps me now with pulse of noisy tears,
Who strikes the breast?
If I forget among the flowing weed,
My regret is
Not vocal, cannot pierce to hidden day,
Momentary, soon quenched, like a strangled flame.'

PETER QUENNELL

DIVERS

Clad in thick mail he stumbles down the floor
    Of the dark primaeval ocean;—on his head
    A casque more gross than ever helmeted
Crusader against Saracen. Before
His glass-dimmed eyes dart shapes like fiends of yore,

Or like malignant spirits of the dead,
To snatch and snap the line where through is fed
A meagre air to that strange visitor.
Stumbling we grope and stifle here below
In the gross garb of this too cumbering flesh,
    And draw such hard-won breaths as may be
    drawn,
Until, perchance with pearls, we rise and go
    To doff our diver's mail and taste the fresh,
    The generous winds of the eternal dawn.

ROBERT HAVEN SCHAUFFLER

INDEX OF TITLES

(Titles in italics indicate works from which selections have been taken.)

INDEX OF AUTHORS

131

INDEX OF FIRST LINES

Deep in the wave is a coral grove,   82
Diver go down   124
Diving for wrecks or sunken treasure, see   125

Evening on the olden, the golden sea of Wales,   90

Falls from her heaven the Moon, and stars sink burning   126
First there were two of us, then there were three of us,   42
Full fathom five thy father lies;   72

Here at the turning of the tide,   80

I am a sea-shell flung   59
I have heard a voice of broken seas   114
I have seen   57
I have sinuous shells of pearly hue   57
I saw a frieze on whitest marble drawn   67
I saw the long line of the vacant shore,   3
I thought of life, the outer and the inner,   56
If when I come to Paradise   70
In sea-cold Lyonesse,   91
In some green island of the sea,   89
In the days before the high tide   12
In this water, clear as air,   84
It is a wonder foam is so beautiful.   7
It keeps eternal whisperings around   3

Leagues, leagues over   101
Leaning on the unpainted rail   22
Leviathan drives the eyed prow of his face,   35
Lo! Death has reared himself a throne   92
Lord, lord! methought what pain it was to drown;   74

Meekly the sea   10
Memory, out of the mist, in a long slow ripple   44
Mermaids six or seven,   103
My cabinets are oyster-shells,   113
My gentle Puck, come hither. Thou rememberest   104

Neptune, besides the sway   114
Now is it pleasant in the summer-eve,   84

O lonesome sea-gull, floating far   41
Of Neptune's empire let us sing,   112
Oh! hush thee, my baby, the night is behind us,   29
On Kennack Sands the sun   104
On the wave-washed scarp of crag   45

Perched on my city office stool   122
Prayer unsaid, and mass unsung,   71

133

Rain, with a silver flail;   18
Roll on, thou deep and dark blue Ocean—roll!   2
Run seaward, launch upon the air, and sound your desolate cry   42

Sabrina fair,   116
Sea-weed sways and sways and swirls   76
See how he dives   25
See what a lovely shell   58
Sleeplessly circle the waves   76
Slow sail'd the weary mariners and saw,   96
Some would dive in the lagoon   121

The broad beach,   44
The delicate shells lay on the shore;   68
The fierce musical cries of a couple of sparrow hawks hunting on the
    headland   46
The fishermen say, when your catch is done   37
The long-rolling,   11
The sea awoke at midnight from its sleep,   4
The sea laments   14
The six-foot nest of the sea-hawk,   48
The snow lies sprinkled on the beach,   5
The world below the brine;   75
There was an island in the sea   88
There's big waves and little waves,   13
These are my murmur-laden shells that keep   68
This is the sea. In these uneven walls   82
This is the ship of pearl, which, poets feign,   64
Thou who hast slept all night upon the storm,   49
Toward the sea turning my troubled eye,   32

Waves that are white far out   7
We have forgot, who safe in cities dwell,   9
What has the sea swept up?   63
When a great wave disturbs the ocean cold   8
When descends on the Atlantic   77
When the last sea is sailed and the last shallow charted,   72
When the wind is in the thrift   10
When we were building Skua Light—   26
Where the seas are open moor   24
Where you see the undersides of their wings   47
White gulls that sit and float   50
Who could devise   65
Who would be a mermaid fair,   97
Who would be a merman bold,   99
Why does the sea moan evermore?   76
Wind-flicked and ruddy her young body glowed   122

You strange, astonish'd-looking, angle-faced,   17

134